The Introvert Love & Wealth Bundle

2 Books: The Quiet Cupid & The

Lone Wolf Tycoon

The Quiet Cupid

An Introvert's Guide to Winning

in Love, Relationships, and

Marriage

The information in the following pages is broadly considered to be a truthful and accurate account of facts, and as such any inattention, use or misuse of the information in question by the reader will render any resulting actions solely under their purview. There are no scenarios in which the publisher or the original author of this work can be in any fashion deemed liable for any hardship or damages that may befall them after undertaking information described herein.

Additionally, the information found on the following pages is intended for informational purposes only and should thus be considered, universal. As befitting its nature, the information presented is without assurance regarding its continued validity or interim quality. Trademarks that mentioned are done without written consent and can in no way be considered an endorsement from the trademark holder.

ISBN: 978-0-9987936-3-4

TABLE OF CONTENTS

INTRODUCTION

Thank you for obtaining your personal copy of *The Quiet Cupid: An Introvert's Guide to Winning in Love, Relationships, and Marriage.* Congratulations on doing so.

The following chapters will discuss some of the many components of an introverted personality and how those traits and tendencies might affect an introvert's love life. They also go into great detail about how to succeed in love as an introvert. Chapter 1 covers some defining characteristics and common challenges that introverts experience. Chapter 2 examines the dating stage and how to navigate it as an introvert. In chapter 3, readers will learn strategies for developing and managing relationships as an introvert.

You will discover how important understanding and coming to terms with your introverted personality truly is. Understanding oneself will help an individual succeed in love, dating, and marriage. When you have a solid grasp on your personality, you can build on your strengths and identify potential changes to be made.

The final chapter will explore marriage, a huge step in the progression of romantic relationships. Introverts will benefit from navigating marriage differently than their non-introverted peers. In addition, marrying a fellow introvert has the potential to develop into of the most rewarding experiences in this world.

The internet and digital publications market are filled with books, websites, and courses on this topic. However, many of them are targeted at general audiences, thus failing to accommodate for introverted personality types and their unique circumstances. This book seeks to help introverts develop the tools that will bring them success in the world of romantic relationships, including dating and marriage.

CHAPTER 1

SO, YOU'RE AN INTROVERT.

Introverts are known to exude a number of characteristics that often complicate their love lives. That is not to say, however, that introverts have more adversity when it comes to romantic relationships. Rather, like other personality types, introverts are faced with their own unique challenges in the realms of love, relationships, and marriage. Those challenges, which will be explored a little later on in this book, often lead to miscommunications, misunderstandings, and disagreements, all of which can, in turn, lead to arguments and escalations of the conflict.

If you have ever found yourself caught in a relationship in which you felt like your partner was unaccommodating of your specific needs, then you will want to read this book through to the end. Perhaps you just wanted to spend time in the presence and proximity of your partner while each of you just did your own thing, only to have your companion accuse you of being distant and quiet.

Or, maybe you are a more reflective, contemplative introvert. You might like to go into great depth of thought, considering how other people interpret your actions. This can cause anyone to spend obscene amounts of time crafting the perfect text replies, obsessing over the perfect words to type out to their partner. As a result, your partner feels neglected when you fail to reply to them in a timely manner, if at all. This book will show you how to manage your introverted tendencies in such a way that has a positive impact on your love life.

You might also experience the social fatigue that comes along with an introverted personality. For example, you might feel wholly unprepared to interact with people just moments before your first date, simultaneously not wanting to cancel or no-show. This predicament can lead to small anxiety attacks while the introverted person begins to frantically contemplate rescheduling.

Other introverts report enjoying a long-distance relationship, but having serious reservations about spending time with their romantic interest in person because they fear that their quiet personality will come off as standoffish. More introverts still complain about family members making intrusive inquiries as to why they do not spend more time with their long-distance partners.

Some people with introverted personalities have had an otherwise wonderful date take a turn for the worse as soon as the interaction moved to a crowded, loud venue. Such places have the potential to wipe out the energy levels of even the most resilient introverts.

A number of introverts also struggle with getting labeled as "quiet." A number of introverted tendencies can cause an individual to behave in a reserved fashion, but when a peer group assigns a label to one of their own, that label reinforces the behavior that it refers to. For example, after enough people nonchalantly told me, in one way or another, that I am "quiet," I started to realize that I was, in fact, very quiet. I even recall saying to myself after one such conversation, in an accepting tone, "Oh yeah, I guess I am quiet." If enough people tell you that you are quiet, you will start to become more and more quiet as you step into the role that your peer group has assigned to you. The challenge, then, comes about when you have to navigate your own dating life while simultaneously managing the social expectations that your peer group has of you. The contents of this publication seek to help introverted individuals overcome the unique challenges that they face. The love, relationships, and marriage portions of introverts' lives will undergo new perspectives. The manageable methods described in this book will provide insight and tips that give introverts the power to enjoy a dating life that effectively navigates the specific challenges that introverts face.

Challenges That Introverts Face

The unique personality traits of most introverts present them with a series of challenges in the way of romantic relationships. Introverts often know that they exist in this world behaving and thinking in ways that might not make sense to the rest of the population. However, introverts understand one another and recognize the reasoning behind some of their identifiable personality traits, including their own gentle natures, thoughtfulness, desires for privacy, high sensitivity levels, and mysteriousness.

First, introverts have to contend with the fact that they are, in general, more gentle than their extroverted counterparts. In most cases, the willingness and ability to behave in a gentle manner are virtuous. However, when it comes to dating, adopting an overly gentle nature will make it difficult to meet new potential partners. Consider a single adult man who is out at a nightclub, looking to meet his next girlfriend. This man has to contend with the other single men in his proximity as they compete for attention from the attractive females in the venue. As such, the men in the room must take it upon themselves to stand out in such a way that attracts female attention. A man who goes through this kind of situation with an insistence on maintaining a gentle disposition will get lost amongst the other average men who fail to make themselves noticed. Similarly, single women also improve their chances of meeting a partner when they make themselves stand out. Most of the traditional venues that facilitate romantic interaction between single people demand that their inhabitants behave loudly and expressively if they are to succeed in meeting somebody. As such, the need to modify the always-gentle nature of introverts into one that bears a load of charisma presents itself, but can be avoided.

Second, introverted people often allow their own thoughtfulness to get in the way of their romantic endeavors. Many unfortunate introverts report feeling unappreciated when their partners fail to see the value in their thoughtful natures. Not everybody will understand or appreciate a highly thoughtful individual. Your best bet, as an introvert, is to link up with a partner who does. The challenge, then, lies in distinguishing such capable individuals from the rest of the dating pool. Even married couples experience conflict when one partner feels that the other is not coming close to matching their levels of thoughtfulness and consideration.

Third, introverts often struggle in the realm of romance

because they have an intense desire to maintain a level of privacy. Partners of privacy-oriented introverts might feel like the introverted partner has an unwillingness to open up. On the other hand, being private can give you an element of intrigue, as your partners feel enticed to learn about you in small pieces. You might come across like a vault of interesting tidbits that your partner extracts from. However, the fast-paced nature of contemporary society makes being private challenging for romantic relationships; people do not have the patience that they used to. If you make your partner prod you to open up and reveal information about yourself, they may get frustrated and move on to somebody more willing to self-disclose. If somebody is curious about you, do not take that for granted. Your private nature will only charm so long as somebody has a desire to learn about the information that you withhold.

Fourth, introverts often struggle with romantic involvement thanks to the fact that they are more sensitive than the rest of the world. Sensitivity, a trademark characteristic of introverts, makes experiences more meaningful and intense. A sensitive person will allow themselves to wholly experience emotions in ways that other people are incapable of. If a sensitive introvert gets good news, then their whole disposition improves in response. Introverts get great enjoyment out of life's simple pleasures. On the other hand, stressful triggers like loud environments and harsh lighting can make an introvert largely uncomfortable, turning otherwise fun events into challenges. For example, going to a concert, while enjoyable for many, can be unpleasant for introverts because of their sensitivities to jarring bass and flashing lights. Worse yet, not only are introverts sensitive to their environments, they also tend to possess high levels of emotional sensitivity as well. This personality characteristic can lead to misunderstandings when the other person involved in a relationship is unaccommodating of it.

Finally, the mysterious natures of introverts make dating, relationships, and marriage challenging in that mystery creates emotional distance. Not letting other people solve the puzzle that is your personality makes them more likely to feel frustrated and even distrusting. Having a degree of mystery to your personality often creates intrigue and attraction in those who take notice of you. However, as you forge a relationship, your partner will, inevitably, want to know more about you. They will seek to understand what makes you who you are. You cannot keep yourself a mystery forever. You can always maintain a mysterious personality, but you will eventually have to communicate with openness and honesty. Coming to terms with your mysteriousness and using it to your advantage can make this personality trait one of your biggest assets in your dating life if harnessed properly.

Four Types of Introverts

Human introversion takes a number of forms. That number, in fact, is four. Psychologists of recent years are now suggesting that introverts come in multiple varieties: anxious, restrained, thinking, and social. Remembering the acronym ARTS will help you keep these classifications at the forefront of your memory. While the defining traits of these four distinctions make them unique, introverts are united under one common trait: a preference for looking inward.

Anxious introversion takes the form of a tendency to experience anxious thoughts that interfere with daily functions. People who experience anxious introversion prefer solitude over socialization. Their personality characteristics cause self-consciousness and anxiety when in the presence of peers. These individuals have very little confidence in their ability to socialize. Worse yet, in many cases, the anxious feelings cease to dissipate once the individual experiencing them finds solitude. Even when alone, anxious introverts are still prone to the anxious thoughts that distinguish them from other introverts. For example, an anxious introvert may find themselves ruminating over the possibility of a disaster occurring, fretting over an upcoming interview, or sitting in bed and mentally replaying over and over a scenario that they encountered earlier.

Next, restrained introverts, also known as reserved introverts, appear to move at a slower rate cognitively. Restrained introverts tend to take their time and think about what to say before contributing their half of a conversation. Furthermore, they have trouble moving into a working state immediately after waking up. Restrained introverts need time to get moving before they can be expected to concentrate or otherwise function optimally. Like an athlete needs to warm up with light exercise before going into a full-on training routine, a restrained introvert needs to warm up before going into full-force socialization or work.

Moving along, thinking introverts enjoy self-reflection and introspection. What sets them apart from other introverts is their lack of distaste for social situations and events. Thinking introverts, in general, have no problem socializing and meeting people. Rather, their introversion takes the form of deep thought and lengthy reflection. The contents of thinking introverts' thoughts differentiate them from the aforementioned anxious introverts. While anxious introverts tend to focus their thoughts on what might go wrong, thinking introverts tend to dwell on more creative, imaginative thoughts.

Lastly, social introverts fit the profile of the stereotypical introvert, if there is such a thing. They prefer to mingle in very small groups or one-on-one. Large group socialization is undesirable for these people. Sometimes, however, social introverts would rather avoid socializing at all. They are perfectly content staying home and enjoying a book or movie. This is different from anxious introversion in that anxiety, while it may be present, does not influence the preference to avoid large groups. The desire to remain in small groups of close friends does not always imply shyness.

Determining the type of introversion that riddles your personality will help you better understand yourself and your unique needs. Introversion's signs and symptoms extend beyond the preference to avoid large crowds. Labeling someone an introvert can make that person feel misunderstood or oversimplified. Introversion is a complex personality trait that is just as complicated as the lives and personalities of those who exude it.

Common Traits of Introverts

Even though introversion takes four different forms, introverts still share a more or less ubiquitous set of traits that signify an introverted personality. Some are positive; others are found to be a hindrance. In this section, we will examine the personality traits that hint at introversion. If you find yourself experiencing a large percentage of the traits described in this section, then you might be an introvert.

First, being socially active drains introverts. Introverts are unique from extroverted and balanced personalities in that they have to expend a great deal of mental energy on social activity. Extroverts are motivated and energized by socialization; introverts are drained and exhausted by it. Individuals with introverted personalities often leave parties and events a bit earlier than the majority of the crowd because they run out of social energy before most others do. In the absence of a place to escape to, some introverts will zone out after a long period of interpersonal interaction.

Second, introverts are drawn and attracted to extroverts. Introverts often look at extroverts with a sense of admiration at their ability to forget about being serious. Extroverts have a lot to offer introverts in terms of fun and new experiences. The old stereotype that opposites attract holds true in the realm of introversion and extroverted personality types.

Third, introverts experience seemingly nonstop self-talk. The frequency of the inner dialogue or monolog that takes place within your mind can indicate your personality type. If you are constantly interacting with the voice in your head, that might suggest that you are an introvert. Extroverts do not go through the same internal considerations that introverts do. Introverts feel a need to thoroughly think before acting, and the self-talk in their heads helps them make such considerations.

Fourth, environmental surroundings do not affect introverts nearly as much as they do extroverts. Introverts are less motivated by their environments. Studies suggest that extroverts associate strong dopamine rushes with their environments. Introverts simply tend not to process their environment in such a way that makes it rewarding. As a result, introverts have less regard for the effects of their environment. For example, if you have been less than enthused over a venue or location that your companion insisted was amazing, then you are likely introverted.

Fifth, introverts enjoy abstract conversations. While details also intrigue introverts, those details mean nothing to an introvert if he or she cannot fathom how those details contribute to a bigger picture. As such, introverts like to establish an abstract main idea and then support that abstraction with concrete details.

Sixth, introverts like to excel at one thing more than trying their hand at everything. The brain patterns that introverts possess cause them to focus on one concept and engage with all facets of that idea. As a result, introverts tend to develop mastery in specific, concentrated fields and abilities. They enjoy the ability to become an expert in anything but often lack the willingness to engage with unfamiliar experiences or skills.

Seventh, introverts tend to be particularly prone to distraction. While extroverts struggle to contain themselves in the absence of something to do, introverts behave in a directly opposite fashion. When faced with multiple options regarding how to spend time, introverts often shut down to the point of unproductivity. Introverts require a work environment that is free of distracting stimulation. Something as trivial as a light being too bright can distract an introvert's thoughts.

Eighth, introverts excel at public speaking. While mingling with their audience members afterward might be daunting, introverts have a marked ability to hold an audience's attention. You are probably an introvert if you would unquestionably prefer to deliver a speech in front of hundreds than talk to those same people in an interpersonal fashion.

Ninth, seemingly trivial interpersonal interactions like networking and small talk are unappealing to introverts. Introverts like to indulge in deeper topics. As a result, small talk conversations prove cumbersome for those afflicted with introverted personalities. Introverts would rather break past the façade that small talk creates and dive into weightier topics of conversation. Similarly, networking feels incredibly phony to introverts. Networking, the process of conversing with the intent of making career connections, comes across as an attempt to get something out of another individual rather than connect with them.

Tenth, pay attention to your choice of seating when in public. Because introverts dislike being surrounded by people, they often choose to sit at the ends of benches. Similarly, introverts are the first to claim aisle, window, and back row seats in classrooms, public transportation, and theaters.

Eleventh, introversion can affect one's choice of live entertainment. Introverts do not like to shine attention on themselves unless the situation demands it. For example, an introverted performing artist will have no problem putting attention on themselves for the durations of their shows. However, introverts believe that live shows are all about the performers onstage. As such, they go out of their way to avoid attending live events that might involve audience participation.

Twelfth, introverts develop their own working cycles that alternate between socialization and solitude or work. The fact that introverts need time to recharge from social activity dictates that they maintain a balance of isolation and outgoingness. As such, many introverts will spend weeks at a time focusing on what seems like nothing but their work and individual hobbies, only to suddenly go out socializing several nights a week for a few weeks. The cycles that introverts maintain are developed in attempts to accommodate the unique needs that those with this personality type possess.

Thirteenth, introverts often do not get the credit that they deserve. One strength of introversion is that it gives people the capacity to be incredibly humble. However, that strength can quickly turn into a downside if an introvert does not consciously make their contributions known. Introverts often fail to see the importance in receiving credit for their work, particularly in the workplace. As a result, they often get overshadowed by those who go out of their way to promote their own efforts.

Fourteenth, the phone calls of introverts often go unanswered, even those that come from loved ones. Introverts will not pick up the phone if they are not in a talkative state. When an introvert chooses to place themselves in solitude, they do so because they feel a need to disconnect from human interaction. Ironically, then, your best chances of getting ahold of an introvert over the phone happen when you call them while they are away from home. Introverts screen calls regularly. (On that note, if you call a marked introvert and they do not answer, leave them a message and allow them to return your call at a time that is comfortable to them.)

Fifteenth, introverts tend to enjoy driving alone. Slow traffic will make any sane person lose their mind for a hot second, but open road conditions are an introvert's haven. The combination of solitude, an engaging activity, and their favorite music makes driving alone therapeutic and enjoyable for introverted individuals. When introverts get overwhelmed, long, relaxing drives can put them at ease.

Sixteenth, recent innovations in technology have afforded Westerners the ability to order prepared food over the internet, a feature that introverts love. When faced with the choice, an introvert will choose to order their meal online before they even think about calling the store.

Seventeenth, introverts often sport headphones in public. Headphones signal to the rest of the world that the individual wearing them would prefer to be left alone. An adaptation, the use of headphones as a tool for deterring unwanted conversations has made itself a common practice of introverts. Some even go so far as to wear headphones plugged into nothing; they just want to be left alone.

Eighteenth, introverts are spotted reading in public places. Going out in public is often an uncomfortable experience for individuals with introverted personalities. Books give them a reason to divert their attention away from any potential social activity that might make an unwelcome entrance into their experiences. When faced with an obligation to endure a public outing, introverts sometimes resort to books as their preferred activity while they wait for their companions to finish going about their business.

Lastly, introverts have to contend with the opinions and labels that others assign them. Introverts report being told that they need to come out of their shell or participate more in class, for example. Many introverted individuals also contend with the labels like "quiet," "snobbish," "old soul," and "intense."

You can say with much certainty that you are an introvert if you find that the majority of traits detailed in this section apply to you and your personality. It is entirely possible that an introvert will not display or possess one-hundred percent of these distinguishing traits, but that does not change the fact that these characteristics suggest introversion.

CHAPTER 2

DATING

For our purposes, dating refers to the processes of seeking, meeting, interacting with, and going out on dates with potential romantic partners before committing to a relationship.

Vs. Extroverts

As an introvert, you may have compared yourself to extroverts in the past. Extroverts, after all, seem to get all of the attention, especially from the other single people in proximity. They appear to have the ability to flirt and mingle with ease. As a result, you may have been led to believe that you have to compete in an uphill battle with extroverts for attention from potential mates. Facing such competition from your perspective can get discouraging and overwhelming. Thankfully, you do not have to compete with extroverts for the attention of other single people. You can (and should)

27

embrace your introverted personality and still meet the partner of your dreams.

Especially extroverted people can be attractive because they are comfortable interacting with others because *that is who they are.* If you try to fake extroversion, you will probably come off as incongruent, forced, and weird. Furthermore, if you do establish yourself as an extrovert, you will have to maintain that façade whenever you are in the presence of the people you first behaved in an extroverted fashion towards. Imagine meeting your long-term partner while you faked extroversion, only to have them expect that out of you every time you interact! You can still be introverted and attractive, but this will require that you come to terms with your introversion.

The most attractive introverts (and other people in general) are comfortable with their personalities. Introverted individuals sometimes struggle to find a date because they do not understand the extent of what they can offer somebody else. In other words, such introverts do not feel like they can live up to the standards of potential partners. The most romantically successful introverts embrace their traits and are therefore able to display those traits in such a way that makes them attractive and alluring. So, the first step to achieving dating success as an introvert involves identifying your unique strengths and then figuring out how to make them work for you. In the following section, we will detail the assets that introverts can bring to a romantic relationship.

Strengths of Being an Introvert

First and foremost, introverts are overwhelmingly more self-sufficient than the rest of the population. Whereas extroverts seek external validation, introverts have the uncanny ability to turn inward for confirmation. As such, you have the capacity to lead a relationship, even when your partner doubts your ability to do so. You have the potential to handle relationship conflicts objectively, even if your partner criticizes and blames you for the disagreement. Without a pressing need to gain the approval of others in your way, you can spend more efforts cultivating and managing your relationships.

However, even before entering into a committed relationship, you have a wealth of opportunities to make your quiet personality shine. People who date introverts often praise their respective partners' abilities to remain calm and cool. Because introverts are comfortable without attention and limelight, they are easy to hang out with. Today's rushed, fame-seeking society makes introversion appealing in contrast. If you can convey, subtly, to a potential mate that your chilled out, easy nature can give them a break from the fast-paced world that you live in, then you can give the impression that you are an attractive choice of partners.

Furthermore, introverts are very careful about the words that come out of their mouths. Because introverts spend a fair amount of time considering their words before uttering them, they are less likely to say something regrettable. Many introverts will not speak at all unless they deem it worthwhile to do so. As such, you, as an introvert, are unlikely to say something that will embarrass a partner. Do not make adjustments to this aspect of your personality in attempts to connect with a partner. When conversing with potential mates, you should display your ability to speak with consideration. Hold a conversation, but do not say anything more than you normally would in that situation. Keep your side of the conversation just word-heavy enough to intrigue your potential mate and make them want to know more about you.

In addition, introverts are known for their ability to be incredibly tenacious, a trait that many people desire in a partner. Introverts are able to dedicate themselves to one task and see it through to completion. For example, one introvert reports getting cut from his girlfriend's school's marching band because he did not march according to their standards. He had transferred to that school in order to be nearer to his partner. Rather than lament over the fact that the band leader ignored his musical abilities, this introverted individual took it upon himself to scrutinize and study the marching patterns of the band that he wanted to be a part of. Because the school's band insisted that all members march according to very precise directions, many people failed to make it past the first round of tryouts. However, our hero in this story was able to meticulously learn and eventually memorize the band's preferred marching patterns. As a result, he was brought into the band after he tried out again the next year. Similarly, you have the capacity to manage relationships with the same resolve. You can and are willing to examine weak points in your relationships and strengthen them. If you are unsure of how to do so, you will have no trouble researching the relationship problem and its solutions. After all, the fact that you picked up this book is already a testament to your studious tenacity.

Next, the intellectually stimulating nature of introverts makes them attractive choices of romantic partners. Introverts dislike small talk because they prefer to dive into more stimulating topics of conversation. This part of their personality can repel those who expect a "normal" conversation with potential mates; however, introverts have a lot to offer in terms of intellectual stimulation. Because introverts spend a lot of time in states of self-reflection, they develop the capacity to deeply explore ideas. Demonstrate this capacity to a potential mate by diving deep into a conversation *about them*. When you are able to convey that you understand another person on a deeper level, or that you are at least able to, you become more attractive in their eyes. Nobody wants a partner who does not "get" them. Your introversion can be your best asset when it comes to demonstrating your natural strengths, including the ability to explore, grasp, and understand the deeper, more subtle aspects of other people. As an added bonus, your potential partners will feel like they do not have to "come clean" if you can communicate that you already have an idea of how they think and act. Make use of your introverted analytical skills and apply them to the lives of the people with whom you converse.

Also, introverts are excellent listeners. Most introverts listen way more than they speak, which often earns them the label of "quiet." However, your listening capabilities are probably some of your best assets when it comes to dating, relationships, and marriage. The extroverts of the world are usually preoccupied with their own lives and obligations, and rightfully so. However, active listening, the process of listening to another person with the intent to understand and empathize, is an incredibly attractive practice. When partners actively listen to one another, the connection between them strengthens. Listen not just to reply, but to engage as well.

Moreover, introverts possess a great capacity for divergent thinking. In other words, they are creative. The act of existing in a state of solitude for extended periods of time breeds creativity. While in solitude, humans are more likely and abler to focus deeply, think outside of the box, and act creatively. Creativity is an attractive trait. Consider the fact that our tribal ancestors contended with problems that they had never heard of with no way of researching how to deal with such a problem. For example, a migrating herd of predatory cats might have made their way into a village for the first time, leaving that tribal neighborhood's inhabitants to figure out a way to deal with the foreign non-human invaders. Tribespeople who could not improvise a defense against aggressive sabretooth tigers would die, while those who successfully survived unheard of problems passed down their creative genes. As such, creativity has evolutionary survival implications and, therefore, is an attractive trait.

Moving on, introverts are blessed with independent natures. If you can subtly demonstrate your capacity for independence to a potential mate, you stand to make yourself more attractive. While having a partner present when you need support is wonderful, nobody wants a partner who is wholly dependent on them. In addition, your independent nature suggests to potential partners that you can at least take care of yourself, which hints that you just might be able to care for a partner when they need you the most. You can demonstrate the resolve and extent of your independent nature by telling a story about a time when you had to fend for yourself while overcoming adversity. For example, I like to bring up how I took on a second job while attending college full time to help pay my hospital bills after I dislocated my elbow four years into my sports entertainment career, which I worked very hard to establish. You get the point.

Lastly, introverts have an amazing tendency to take care of their own well-beings. You might not want to make yourself stand out amongst a crowd, but you can still go out of your way to rise above the competition in terms of cleanliness and overall health and appearance. Introverts know the value of maintaining a healthy body. Solitude helps people develop a meticulous self-care routine. For example, introverts are often seen wearing nice clothing while well-groomed. They are like less noticeable models. When you go out of your way to take care of yourself, potential mates will notice. Again, the ability to care for yourself implies an ability to care for a partner when they need you. In contrast, if you fail to maintain certain grooming and hygiene standards, otherwise potential partners will be repelled. If you cannot care for yourself, how can anyone expect you to care for them when they need you to? Demonstrate your uncanny ability to take care of yourself; put effort towards hygiene, grooming, and dressing well.

In sum, you can harness your introverted qualities and tendencies in such a way that promotes your most attractive offerings. Namely, your self-sufficiency, calm composure, careful manner of speaking, tenacity, intellectual stimulation capabilities, active listening skills, creativity, independent nature, and self-care abilities can make you a catch in the eyes of potential mates. Next, we will explore how you can go about seeking and meeting a partner with those considerations in mind.

Dating Tips for Introverts

Dating is hard enough without introvert tendencies tripping you up along the way. This section is designed to help introverts achieve success in their dating lives through practical, applicable tips that are often situation-specific.

First, parties are a great place to meet your next fling. However, introverts go about parties differently than the rest of the population does. While extroverted partygoers see parties as opportunities to socialize with new people and make a great number of new connections, introverts prefer to enjoy the company of the people that they already know. As a whole, the introverted population does not enjoy parties any more or less than the extroverts do; they just enjoy them differently. As such, introverts should attend parties without comparing their social activity to extroverts because to do so would be a losing battle against one's own insecurities.

Instead, introverts must accept that they are, in fact, introverted and plan to party accordingly. To illustrate, introverts feel better about parties when they plan to attend, but only for a small amount of time. Instead of partying all night until the booze is gone, consider only mingling for two hours or so with the intention of moving your social activity elsewhere with a smaller group. For example, if you plan on attending a party with friends, make plans with them ahead of time to leave the gathering to go out to eat at a certain time in the evening. Then, if you meet a potential mate at the party, you can invite that person to join you and your friends in a small-group context that you are more comfortable in.

Second, consider online dating. Introverts tend to be more proficient with written communication than oral, face-to-face communication. Therefore, online dating makes an optimal choice of partner-finding media. Capitalize on your written communication skills and seek partners digitally. In addition, your online mate-meeting endeavors are not limited to dating platforms. You can also meet people on forums, message boards, and social media platforms. Alex Plank, the founder of wrongplanet.net, a popular online forum for discussing autism and autism-related issues, reports that many married couples originally met on his website. While you may not be immediately seeking a spouse, this anecdote serves as evidence of the fact that online communication can facilitate romantic relationships.

Third, open yourself up to casual conversation. It is well-established at this point that introverts at least dislike small talk. However, that is not a reason to dismiss its potential to develop into something more. Many people meet their spouse during chance conversations that they never expect to turn into anything beyond a friendly, one-off interaction.

Fourth, try to focus your attention away from yourself. This can be difficult for anyone, especially those who are accustomed to spending time engaged in self-reflection. However, when you go about your dating life overly focused on yourself, you distract yourself from the task at hand: finding out if the person in your presence might be worth building a future with. So, the next time you find yourself at a social gathering, pick out one person in the room and make a point to find out more about them. You already know a lot about yourself; take yourself out of your mental spotlight. Think "there you are" instead of "look at me."

Fifth, place yourself in positions to meet people in environments that you find comfortable. Many introverts hate the prospect of enduring crowded clubs and bars in exchange for the chance to talk to somebody who might or might not be worth knowing. Thankfully, more comfortable alternatives to dating exist. Consider investing time in a hobby that facilitates interpersonal interaction. For example, you might get involved with art classes, volunteer opportunities, or team sports and athletic endeavors. These activities give you the chance to meet people organically and expand your social network so that you might meet a partner without subjecting yourself to uncomfortable environments and situations.

To summarize, finding and meeting a date does not have to be a puzzle for introverts. Simple, concrete adjustments to your approach can make the difference between a successful outing and a return home without a date lined up. So, to make the most of your social opportunities, plan your partying in an accommodating fashion, try your hand at meeting others online, embrace small talk, shine attention completely away from yourself, and put yourself in situations that will help you meet people in ways that work for you.

Your Dating Life

You cannot avoid going on dates. Dating is the primary means by which relationships form. Your introverted personality might make you dread the idea of spending extended time with another person, but you definitely have to do it if you want to meet a romantic partner. Thankfully, unless you live in a country that oppresses the rights of certain genders and ethnic groups, you have the right to determine your own boundaries in this process. You are not obligated to choose any one course of action throughout your dating endeavors. For example, if you find that going on more than one date in a two-week period is too draining, you can limit the number of dates that you agree to go on.

On that note, you must take care to avoid experiencing dating related FOMO. Also known as fear of missing out, FOMO happens to people when they feel left out or left behind with regards to the activities of their peer groups. So, you might experience FOMO if you see one or more of your friends going out on multiple dates in one weekend, posting couples pictures on social media, and so on. Understand that you and the members of your social circles and networks have unique, different personalities. What might be suitable for one person's dating life could be counterproductive for another's. If you have an introverted personality, you might find yourself overwhelmed if you agree to go on more dates than you can handle, especially if interpersonal interaction has the potential to wipe you of your mental energy. As such, adhere to a dating calendar that works for you and your personality.

Along those same lines, if you feel like rescheduling a date would improve your chances of making a good impression when the date does happen, then do that. You might find yourself unable to muster up the energy and shine required to engage with another individual. Worse yet, your date is scheduled to take place in seven hours. If a situation like this ever happens to you, your best bet is to call your date and inform them that you wish to reschedule. You do not have to offer a drawn-out explanation or detailed reason, but you should make it clear that you do want to go on the date, only at a later time. Ignore any FOMO and take care of your own needs first.

Finding Fellow Introverts

Relationships between introverts tend to work because both parties understand the personality traits of one another to a large degree. Introverted couples can get away with not needing to compromise their personalities in order to accommodate the needs of one another. As such, your most fulfilling relationship might bloom out of a date with a fellow introvert.

If you happen to find yourself single at a party, then you could very well meet your next partner there! When mingling at a party, try seeking out fellow introverts. Introverts are easy to spot; people with introverted personalities display a number of recognizable behaviors at parties. Namely, they remain along perimeters and exclude themselves from large groups. Much like their extroverted counterparts, introverts do enjoy and benefit from socializing and mingling. However, they go about those activities differently than extroverts do. While extroverts tend to congregate in large, centrally located groups at parties, introverts tend to huddle up in small groups or pairs, usually near the edges of rooms. Additionally, introverted party attendees might be seen entertaining themselves with activities that do not involve interacting with other people, such as playing with a pet, grazing the snack table, or watching any live musicians that might be performing. If you spot a fellow introvert at a party, strike up a conversation with them. If your introvert-spotting abilities are to be trusted, your new acquaintance will probably be happy to fast-forward through small talk and delve into more meaningful subjects.

In addendum, many introverts enjoy hosting parties and would prefer to do so instead of attending another person's. Hosting has a wealth of benefits that introverts desire, including the ability to determine the party's hours, attendees, and environment. Hosts have the capacity to manipulate parties to a degree so that they feel comfortable in what would otherwise seem like an overwhelming scenario. Hosting allows introverts the opportunity to socialize in a party atmosphere while reducing the risk of experiencing uncomfortable uncertainties and variables. In addition, hosts have a valid reason to escape conversations if they feel the need to; their hosting obligations can pull them away from an interaction at a moment's notice. So, you might have success meeting a fellow introvert if you take it upon yourself to get to know the host. In addition, hosting your own party or parties will afford you opportunities to meet people in a controlled environment of your liking. Consider hosting a social gathering if you have the means to do so. Encourage your friends to invite their friends. If you have trouble making a sufficient guest list, consider publicizing your party on social gathering platforms like Meetup and Eventbrite.

Thankfully, your chances of encountering fellow introverts are great in environments that do not contain large crowds or expectations of social interaction. For example, many introverts, single ones included, enjoy spending time in nature. The great outdoors offers introverts the opportunity to get away from overwhelming crowds of people and explore the world at their own leisure. Consider joining a club that facilitates nature exploration endeavors like hikes and trail walks. Because of the nature-loving tendencies of introverts, many such organizations are overflowing with introverted personality types. Outdoor clubs facilitate and encourage interaction between members, eliminating or at least reducing the awkwardness that comes with approaching strangers outside of social gatherings. Even if nature is not necessarily your thing, joining such a club will improve your chances of meeting a fellow introvert and give you opportunities to explore environments you may have never thought to visit on your own.

Seeing Through Pseudo-Extroverts

Many well-meaning introverts successfully disguise themselves as extroverts. They do so because they have a desire to possess the outgoing nature of extroverts, so they effectively mimic extroverted personality traits. A seemingly extroverted person might, in fact, be an introvert disguised as the opposite personality type. When an introvert takes on a number of extroverted behaviors, they do so because they have an intense desire to experience the same social experiences that extroverts enjoy. As such, pseudo-extroverts are usually, on the surface, open to interactions with many individuals. As an introvert, you have a great chance of striking up a conversation and deeply connecting with a pseudo-introvert. Recognizing and knowing the telltale signs of pseudo-extroverts will help your chances of meeting them.

First, pseudo-extroverts tend to zone out, especially in the midst of heavy social interaction. Introverts, as you know by now, tend to get overwhelmed by populated social situations. Pseudo-extroverts cope with this tendency by zoning out. Spacing out affords them the opportunity to block out external stimuli and gather their bearings. Somebody who alternates between periods of intense socializing and silent daydreaming is likely a pseudo-extrovert.

Second, introverts in disguise tend to leave parties earlier than the rest of the attendees. Pseudo-extroverts like to mingle at parties before the events go into full swing. They get a sudden uncomfortableness to when party attendees get too involved for their preferences. If you notice somebody who regularly leaves a party early, despite seeming to have a great time socializing, consider approaching them as if they were a pseudo-extrovert.

Third, these disguised personalities will often be found remaining close to a small number of select individuals throughout the course of the event. Introverts at heart, pseudo-extroverts cannot avoid some of their natural tendencies, including the desire to stay in the company of familiar individuals.

Such individuals also tend to demonstrate a special fascination with the artwork, literature, and unique décor found at the party's environment. They tend to give extra attention to pets and prefer to help out with less social tasks like disk jockeying, cleaning, and preparing food. If you spot an attractive pseudo-extrovert at a social gathering, approach them! They have the learned ability to hold a social interaction and simultaneously connect with fellow introverts in ways that they cannot with extroverts.

Avoid Alcohol

Alcohol, often hailed in the dating world as a "social lubricant," can have disastrous effects for introverts in particular. Most people are aware of alcohol's ability to turn anyone, introverted or not, into an obnoxious nuisance. However, introverts face another risk when they drink during the dating process: losing the ability to determine if the other person is right for them.

As an introvert, you probably take great care to only let the most real, most thoughtful people into your life. Alcohol impairs your ability to judge the characters of others. As such, it is to be avoided if you intend to exercise a degree of selectivity when determining the potential of a future with your date. As an introvert, you likely go through dating with much more selectivity than your extroverted peers.

Furthermore, alcohol is often abused as a crutch. If you depend on alcohol to loosen you up to the point of sociability, you are teaching yourself to depend on a foreign substance. And, as you probably already know, dependence is an early point on the path to addiction.

So, your best bet as an introvert is to avoid consuming alcohol, especially on your first date with somebody. Opt for caffeinated non-alcoholic beverages instead. They will still promote a talkative nature, but will not impede on your ability to effectively judge the character of your date. After all, you just might end up spending the rest of your life with this person. Allow yourself to get to know your date so that you do not end up choosing the wrong lifelong partner later.

CHAPTER 3

RELATIONSHIPS

The relationship stage, defined for our purposes as the period of courtship that takes place between dating and marriage, requires active management and a willingness to compromise. As an introvert, you will have to contend with your unique skills and challenges that comprise your personality. Navigating a relationship as an introvert has its upsides as well as its disadvantages.

Advantages of Introversion in Relationships

As an introvert, you can offer partners certain advantages that extroverts cannot. Introverts usually thrive in relationships that are established beyond the dating phase. In other words, committed, exclusive one-on-one romantic relationships are an introvert's specialty. Connecting deeply with one special individual makes itself much easier for introverts than meeting and interacting with relative strangers. As such, introverts interested in romantic relationships should understand the strengths that they bring to committed relationships.

First, introverts can provide their partners with a relaxing space. Introverts, usually quiet and reserved in nature, handle relationships with a cool demeanor. Extroverted partners of introverts report enjoying the calming influence that their partners have on them.

Second, introverts are comfortable letting their respective partners have the spotlight. This is especially beneficial for introverts in relationships with extroverted partners. Introverts tend not to get jealous when their respective partners get attention from others who might even be interested in them. Most introverts are confident enough in their own worth to avoid worrying about their partner taking center stage and leaving them in the dark at times. In fact, some introverts even prefer such an arrangement, living vicariously through their respective partners' experiences. As such, introverts possess the uncanny ability to confidently sit back while their respective partners enjoy the limelight.

Third, most introverts are great at learning from their own mistakes and taking steps to avoid committing those same errors in the future. Because introverts value peace and quiet, they develop an incredible capacity to reflect on and come to terms with their own shortcomings. For example, if an introvert wrongfully says something hurtful to their partner out of anger and spite, they are usually quick to realize their mistake and admit to it. The amount of self-reflection that introverts do contributes to this strength of theirs. Introverts place value on traits like integrity and thoughtfulness. The prospect of a romantic partner who can easily admit when they are wrong appeals to the vast majority of people.

Similarly, introverts possess the strength of care. They excel at empathizing with and understanding the needs and emotions of others. This trait manifests itself in an ability to deeply connect with a partner. Awareness of your partner's thoughts and feelings will give you the perspective needed to understand them more completely.

As a result of their careful nature, introverts also have a strong ability to build great levels of rapport with romantic partners. Introverts are less interested in trivial topics of discussion like current events and weather; they prefer to get involved in more "real" conversations. Rapport strengthens relationships. Thankfully, introverts excel in that area, thanks in no small part to their patient natures. Introverts, in their desire to get into deep conversation, are usually the ones who help make the sometimes uncomfortable transition to heavier topics of conversation that build strong rapport. For example, introverts typically take it upon themselves to move into touchy topics of conversation like morals, sexuality, and religious allegiances. While sensitive, the attitudes that partners have on these subjects have the potential to make or break a relationship. Moreover, they will eventually have to arise as a romantic relationship progresses. Thankfully, introverts know just how to bring up these topics without putting undue pressure on the situation.

Finally, committed romantic relationships are great for introverts in that honesty takes a front seat. Crucial to the health of any relationship, honesty is an introvert's strong suit. Introverts despise the drama and conflict that dishonesty has the potential to cause. As a result, introverts tend to be more honest with their partners than their extroverted counterparts are. Introverts do not enjoy hiding who they are.

As an introvert, you have a lot that you can bring to a romantic relationship. Recognizing your strengths and abilities is crucial to understanding how you contribute to such an arrangement. Remember, introverts provide partners with a calm nature, lack of jealousy, error correction capabilities, care, rapport, and honesty.

Introvert-Introvert Relationships

Introvert-introvert relationships, or romantic arrangements between pairs of introverts, often work better than do relationships between individuals of varying personality types. The previous chapter provided suggestions for finding and meeting another introvert; this section will detail the potential benefits that such relationships provide in addition to suggestions for managing such a relationship.

The primary upside of dating another introvert comes in the form of an intuitive understanding between the two of you. Introverts have an easier time making their needs known to other introverts. Nonverbal communication between introverts is usually less ambiguous than nonverbal communication between, say, and introvert and an extrovert.

First, be okay with it if your partner wants to stay at home while you go out. There will inevitably be times where you have a disagreement regarding whether to stay home or leave the house. When each person can do their own thing without guilt or obligation, introvert-introvert relationships flourish. Similarly, let your partner go out and enjoy a night out while you stay at home if you want to stay in. However, on the occasion that the both of you want to either go out or stay in together, enjoy yourselves.

Second, share uncomfortable responsibilities evenly. As introverts, you and your introverted partner probably have reservations about performing tasks like talking to customer service representatives. When you take turns handling such unfavorable obligations, you maintain a sense of fairness and equality in the relationship. On the other hand, when one partner gets stuck with all of the undesirable responsibilities, resentments often arise. Ensure that your relationship is fair and balanced by evenly dividing up your least favorite tasks. Other less-than-desirable tasks to be divided up might include questioning a salesperson, answering the door for delivery persons, and calling to make a payment or place an order by phone.

Third, make going out fun. Introverts often struggle to convince themselves to leave the house. However, if you can make your regular couple outings more enjoyable, then your relationship will benefit from the fun that you have outside of your home. For example, if you have to go to a networking event, plan a date at your favorite restaurant with your partner that takes place shortly after the end of your obligatory gathering. Or, if you want to go out while your partner insists on staying in, you might try bribing them to leave the house with the promise of a fun experience that they can only have if they go out with you. For example, you might promise to let your partner pick out the movies for your next three at-home movie night dates if they muster up the courage to accompany you to a party. Incentivizing yourselves to exit your comfort zones will help you and your partner handle your out-of-the-house obligations with optimism.

Fourth, pledge to keep all communication honest, direct, and holistic. There may be times in an introvert-introvert relationship where one partner has a hard time interpreting the disposition of the other. Because external triggers can lead to drastic changes in the attitudes of introverts, you might find yourself wondering if your introverted partner's distant attitude is a result of your behavior, for example. If you find yourself in such a situation, do not be afraid to ask your partner about the cause of their slightly off disposition. Of course, you will want to find out whether your partner is upset with you or if they are just displaying their introverted tendencies. Promise to each other to always ask about such uncertainties and that you will not get offended at such questions

Do Not Ignore Your Friends

When a relationship is strong, fresh, and smooth, the partners involved do make efforts to spend as much time with each other as possible, either in person or through digitally mediated communication platforms. Some new parties to a relationship make the mistake of neglecting relationships with friends and family so that they can put more effort into their committed relationships.

However, when and if the romantic relationship comes to an end, the parties involved will benefit from having a strong support system. In other words, after a breakup, humans are best off when their friends are there for them. As such, it is important to maintain somewhat of a relationship with your friends, even when your partner draws all of your attention.

Because introverts tend to keep a small, tightly bonded circle of friends, their needs to maintain those friendships throughout the course of a relationship are doubly important. You do not have to call your friends every day, but a simple text message every so often will let them know that you still think about and value them as friends.

Your close friends do not want to lose you to a new partner, but they should also not demand that you maintain the same commitment to them that you did pre-relationship. Real friends will understand that you have a new partner and, as such, will have reasonably less time for them. However, that is not to suggest that you have permission to wholly ignore your other real-world connections in favor of one sexy individual. Think about who will be there for you if your relationship ends; cherish those people.

Take Care of Your Own Needs

Successful relationships are the ones in which both parties establish their own boundaries, needs, and wants while respecting one another's. The responsibility to communicate the needs of your introverted personality to your partner lies in your hands. Specifically, introverts often require time in solitude. Make it clear to your partner that you need regular alone time, taking care to explain your reasoning. Inform your partner that, as an introvert, you regularly need time to yourself. Articulate that your desire for solo time has nothing to do with a desire to get away from your partner, but rather, stems from a need to recharge in solitude. Reinforce this point until your partner grasps the idea that you would need time away from anybody, not just them specifically. In the event that your romantic partner is extroverted, the requirement for alone time becomes more pressing than it would in an introvert-introvert arrangement.

On the other hand, if you enjoy a romantic relationship with a fellow introvert, then your need for time apart may dissipate or decline. Because introverts understand that silence between them does not suggest distance, they can maintain relationships in which they indulge in alone time while in the presence of one another. For example, many introverted couples enjoy reading or otherwise just hanging out in the same room while they remain largely silent or noninteractive. In any case, determining, communicating, and negotiating your introverted needs is crucial to the long-term success of your romantic relationships.

CHAPTER 4

MARRIAGE

Marriages are unique contractual agreements in that they do not guarantee any sort of outcome. Business contracts and other legally binding agreements guarantee that all parties involved in the negotiations end up with something as soon as the contract takes effect. For example, corporate businesspeople might sign a contract in which one party trades services for money and equity from the other. On the other hand, a marriage contract does not guarantee anything to either party, aside from a few tax and insurance benefits. The unpredictable world of marriage provides great fulfillment to those who navigate it effectively.

Coping with Sleeping Patterns

Introverts, as a whole, possess different sleeping needs than the rest of the population. As a married person, you will be

57

living with another human being. Moving in with a new spouse is akin to getting a new roommate. As such, you and your spouse will have to contend with and accommodate the biological needs of one another. Sleeping arrangements are no exception. This section is designed to help introverts understand and articulate sleeping tendencies that might need to be negotiated as part of a marriage.

In general, introverts require and desire more sleep than their extroverted counterparts. While most extroverts would forgo sleep entirely if they could, introverts welcome the break from full consciousness. Sleep, according to introverts, provides a chance to refresh the mind and escape from the hectic environments that plague their waking daylight hours. As such, you will need to communicate your need for sleep to your partner. Your partner should understand that your elevated sleep requirements do not suggest laziness or other shortcomings on your part; rather, the need to get extra sleep is just a result of your ingrained personality type.

Additionally, introverts find sleep therapeutic. Dreams provide introspective individuals with a chance to explore the depths of their unconscious psyche. Understanding the self is often a relieving experience, especially for those with introverted personality types.

Similarly, introverts tend to stay up and sleep in later than do their extroverted counterparts. The late hours of the day provide a scenario in which introverts thrive: a quiet, slow-paced environment that allows time for distraction-free reflection. Because introverts value introspection, nighttime environments often invigorate their minds. While other people snore, introverts enjoy contemplating and reflecting on past experiences, future considerations, and random assortments of other ponderings. In the night, introverts often get highly engaged with their internal monologs because of the fact that the demands that contemporary working hours place on society do not afford them that opportunity when the sun is out.

You will need to communicate to your spouse that your personality comes equipped with unique sleeping habits that might seem strange or abnormal to regular extroverts. Negotiating sleeping arrangements in your marriage will help you and your spouse get the rest that each of you needs without interfering with the needs of others. If needed, you might have to allow a spouse who goes to sleep early to enjoy a quiet bedroom while you stay awake in another area of the house. While your spouse should respect your natural sleeping habits, you must also respect and accommodate theirs. Do not make them feel guilty for wanting to get some sleep when you would rather they stay up and hang out.

Similarly, if you are accommodating of your spouse's sleeping habits, then you can expect them to refrain from prodding you to wake up before you are ready. Sleep, according to Abraham Maslow, is a basic human need that must be met before a relationship can thrive. Spouses that go through their marriage in a constant state of tiredness will, when all other variables are equal, not enjoy the same quality of marriage as will a well-rested couple.

Prioritize Your Roles

Relationships of all types, social, business, and otherwise, dictate that the parties involved maintain their own roles. For example, a business relationship between two individuals might place one person in the role of supervisor while the other takes on the role of a subordinate. Similarly, you likely have several social and professional roles that you play, including but not limited to romantic partner, parent, student, and friend. As such, it is important that you prioritize your roles so that you afford each of them an appropriate portion of your limited time.

For example, if you are a parent, it would be ill-advised to neglect your young kids in favor of going on a date with a new romantic partner. As such, determining how much priority you place on each of your roles will help determine the overall quality of your life.

As an introvert, you probably value your deepest friendships dearly. So, you might not be so high on the idea of putting them on the back burner to accommodate a new romantic partner. There is no one-size-fits-all prescription for prioritizing the roles that one plays in life. Instead, individuals must determine how they want to run their own lives. This can be a tricky process, as spending an abundance of time in one role might cause others to go neglected.

Thankfully, as an introvert, you likely prefer to maintain a small number of deep relationships over a large number of surface-level ones. This means that your risk of stretching your attention too thin runs lower than the risk levels that your extroverted counterparts face. However, you may have to inform your partner that your children will take priority over them, for example. In any case, take the time to consider how much time and effort you can appropriately dedicate to each of your roles in life. Make adjustments as needed.

Select Carefully

Assuming that you intend to maintain a long-term monogamous relationship, you, as an introvert, need to be more selective than extroverts. Because of your capacity to develop incredibly deep, meaningful rapport, you and your spouse will likely end up revealing a lot about yourselves to one another if your marriage lasts for a while. As such, you will likely end up seeing many sides of your partner and their character that an extroverted person never would. Therefore, many dating columnists advise introverts to exercise an added degree of selectivity when choosing long-term romantic partners.

Do not rush into a committed meaningful relationship with the first person who takes an interest in you. You will need to get a deep understanding of their character and personality before you can commit to that person. Your introversion is a gift and a curse in that you bring out deeply hidden aspects of other people's personalities. With regards to romantic relationships, that means that you will need to be extremely selective if you are to enjoy a successful lifelong commitment with another human being. Do not, however, let the guise of selectivity deter you from pursuing contact with somebody that you think you might have a future with.

You should be sure beyond a shadow of a doubt that your romantic partner is "the one" before you commit to marrying them. The intuition capabilities that your introverted personality has likely blessed you with will assist you in your selectivity.

Encourage Your Spouse to Socialize Elsewhere

I am not suggesting that you tell your partner to leave you alone. Rather, your spouse should understand that they are encouraged to maintain nonromantic relationships outside of the marriage. Encourage your spouse to maintain an active social life that they can enjoy either with or without you. This will allow your spouse the opportunity to have fun while they simultaneously cater to your introverted personality.

As an added benefit, spouses of introverts who keep a social circle outside of the marriage tend to have more fulfilling marriages. When a married person gets the chance to socialize with friends and acquaintances, they are less likely to depend on their spouse for all of their socialization needs. So, a socially active spouse will let you enjoy nights to yourself and keep themselves socially fulfilled at the same time. Never discourage your spouse from going out with their friends, especially when you would rather spend time in solitude. Of course, if you worry about your spouse participating in inappropriate extramarital activities on nights when they let you be alone, then that is a separate issue that your introverted personality is not responsible for.

If your spouse's friends do not have a lot of spare time for socializing with them, encourage more formal social arrangements for them. For example, suggest that they join a club, poker league, or amateur sports team. Any healthy social activity that will keep your spouse entertained while you get your much-needed solitude will help your marriage thrive.

Furthermore, if absence causes the heart to become fonder, then your scheduled solitude will make it that much sweeter when your spouse returns from his or her nights out. If your spouse has an extroverted personality, they will return from their social outings energized and happy to see you while you get to feel refreshed and relaxed from your time alone. Either way, keeping your spouse busy while they afford you solitude will help keep the marriage happy.

Along those same lines, if one spouse wants to go out to an event that you were both invited to as a couple, it is perfectly okay for the other to stay behind. Taking your spouse along with you when they prefer not to come along will cause them to resent you, and vice versa. Let each spouse maintain their autonomy and choose how they spend their free time, so long as they do not violate any of the marriage's expectations along the way.

Find Solitude in Public

It is no secret by now that introverts tend to thrive off of solitude. However, solitude is not limited to time spent alone in the privacy of your own home. Rather, you can find a solitude of sorts out in public. For example, some introverts report feeling refreshed after browsing their local shopping mall with a pair of headphones on. In addition, taking a walk or jog at an outdoor park can provide introverts with the break that they need. It is unfair to expect your spouse to let you have your shared home to yourself every time you need a moment to yourself. As such, you may have to adapt to cohabitation by finding solitude outside of the home. You should not neglect your introverted needs in order to appease a partner. However, you may have to cater to them in innovative ways that you did not consider during your time living without a partner.

Always be Communicating

Communication is an essential component to any healthy relationship, romantic or otherwise. However, without effective communication, a marriage is bound to fail. You and your spouse are unique individuals with unique needs. Communicating the needs that relate to your introverted personality might prove difficult, especially if your spouse does not display many introverted tendencies. Expect that it might take time for a spouse to grasp your introversion and its implications.

Along those same lines, you cannot expect your spouse to accommodate your personality if you fail to adjust to theirs. For example, if you marry an extrovert, understand that they may very well have an intense need to be social. If that is the case, allow them to enjoy nights on the town with large groups of people. Do not feel obligated to come along on your spouse's social outings, but do not try to prevent them from enjoying some harmless socialization with their friends. If your spouse tries to pressure you into going out and the prospect of doing so makes you uncomfortable, communicate with them and inform them of your reservations about large groups of people.

Similarly, do not allow an extroverted spouse pressure you into accompanying them to a social event when you would much rather enjoy some quiet time. It is your responsibility to articulate your need for solitude. A spouse who respects your personality will understand and let you choose how you spend your free time.

So, how do you effectively articulate your introverted needs to your spouse? More importantly, how do you negotiate those needs with the socialization needs of your spouse? You have to be concise, specific, and concrete. You cannot get away with mentioning that you "sometimes need to be alone" and expect that off-handed comment to suffice. What frequency does "sometimes" imply? When you say you need to be "alone," do you need your spouse to just go to another room for fifteen minutes, or do you require hours of solitude without any other people in your vicinity?

Next, come up with a strategy for meeting your needs. You might agree that your spouse will give you the apartment to yourself at least one night a week, for example. Furthermore, you could come to an agreement that allows you to isolate yourself from your spouse for up to two hours without question. Your unique needs will determine the strategies that you craft for going about meeting them.

If seemingly unresolvable communication issues plague the success of your marriage, consider seeking professional couples' therapy.

Take Turns Leading

If you and your spouse's personalities are aligned in such a way that interferes with agreements about your social lives, consider taking turns deciding how to go about social events. For example, your extroverted spouse might insist that you go out and interact with friends as a couple while you prefer to stay at home and enjoy the company of one another. In cases such as this one, switching off the spouse responsible for determining social activity can prove beneficial. Doing so will allow each spouse to experience the world of their partner.

In addition, introducing your spouse to social activities that they are not used to is a great way to help the two of you understand one another. Seeing how your partner likes to socialize will give you great insight into why they are the way that they are.

So, when date night rolls around, determine whose turn it is to pick the date's activity. The spouse in charge of this will get to pick the activity that the two of you partake in for the evening. For example, your spouse might take you to a casino one weekend, leaving you free to choose a movie night at home the next.

CONCLUSION

Thank you for reaching the ending of *The Quiet Cupid: An Introvert's Guide to Love, Marriage, and Relationships*. I sincerely hope that you enjoyed it and found it to be a valuable tool in achieving your love, marriage, and relationship goals, whatever those might be.

The next step is to consciously apply the knowledge offered in the pages of this book to your personal life. Theories and information will only take you so far; the responsibility to make use of your newly acquired perspectives is solely yours. In this book, we discussed introversion and its implications in dating, relationships, and marriages.

If you like to hear about my other projects, please visit the address below.

http://clika.pe/l/13430/56723/

Finally, if you found this book useful in any way, a review on

Amazon is always appreciated! I can only improve this material if you let me know what I'm doing wrong. Think of it as "paying it forward" for the next reader, by letting them know your experience.

The Lone Wolf Tycoon

A Guide for Introverts to Crack the Code to Wealth

The information in the following pages is broadly considered to be a truthful and accurate account of facts, and as such any inattention, use or misuse of the information in question by the reader will render any resulting actions solely under their purview. There are no scenarios in which the publisher or the original author of this work can be in any fashion deemed liable for any hardship or damages that may befall them after undertaking information described herein.

Additionally, the information found on the following pages is intended for informational purposes only and should thus be considered, universal. As befitting its nature, the information presented is without assurance regarding its continued validity or interim quality. Trademarks that mentioned are done without written consent and can in no way be considered an endorsement from the trademark holder.

INTRODUCTION

Congratulations on purchasing your personal copy of *The Lone Wolf Tycoon: A Guide for Introverts to Crack the Code to Wealth*, and thank you for doing so! If you are an introvert who is ready to start capitalizing on the common character traits of your personality, this is your book! In this book, we will examine some of the common character traits of introverts and explore how these characteristics became the building blocks to success that led some famous introverts to make their millions!

The first chapter will cover an overview of what it means to be an introvert, and cover how beneficial this personality type can be in today's marketplace. Some of the most successful entrepreneurs of our time are introverts; this chapter will introduce you to them and the introvert character traits that aided them in securing their wealth and fame.

The second chapter will begin the dissection of character traits listed in the first chapter. Humility, a common character trait of the introverted, will be the focus of this chapter. We will discuss how a quiet voice can roar, and how to be "boldly humble." You will be given an example of how being a calm yet secure person can have a bigger impact on the world than one could ever imagine.

Moving on from humility, the third chapter will discuss how self-sufficiency, another common character trait of the introverted, can become empower one enough to be able to provide for others. Becoming a self-sufficient individual is something that everyone strives for, this chapter will detail why it is so important.

Making the best of solitude is another common character trait of the introverted, and it will be the topic of the fourth chapter. To be introverted is to re-energize while alone. Introverts make the most of their time alone. If you are not already making the best of your alone time, this chapter will inspire you to begin doing so. This chapter will also break down how to budget your life, which is key to financial success.

The fifth chapter will cover the introvert's natural creative tendencies, and what they could mean monetarily. Most introverts have a creative outlet which they enjoy exploring; if this is the case for you, this chapter will give you examples of how best to fan that natural spark into a raging fire.

The sixth chapter will cover being goal oriented, another natural inclination of the introvert. If you are not the super creative type but your planners and calendars could rival that of any CEO, you already have a great natural tendency that can prove extremely lucrative with the right guidance.

Once you are making the best of your alone time, creatively or otherwise, we will discuss how to make the best of your time in public. Chapter seven will cover an introvert's natural inclination for observation. Introverts are very often described as extremely observant in public situations. Instead of focusing on making themselves the center of attention, as is the method of the extrovert, the introvert scans his or her surroundings, analyze everything and making calculations on how best to proceed. This is another of the most profitable traits of the introvert; the chapter will explore this.

Finally, once you have reached your status as a lone wolf tycoon, chapter eight will give you important advice about staying there and thriving as a successful introvert.

It is my genuine hope in writing this book that by the time you get finished reading, you realize your full potential and are inspired by those introverts around you that have tasted great successes. By the time you have reached the end of these pages, you should have a much firmer foundation from which to build your empire!

There are plenty of books on this subject on the market, thanks again for choosing this one! Every effort was made to ensure it is full of as much useful information as possible. Please enjoy!

CHAPTER 1

INTROVERSION AND SUCCESS

O nce upon a time, business was all done face to face. A businessman was gauged on his ability to present himself to his customers and extroverts ruled the business world. Boisterousness was a key to success. One had to be loud to be heard and it was necessary to be in order to be effective. Gregariousness was almost a required trait to be successful in the business realm up until about the 1970s. It was then that things began to change. In this book, we will be all of these things (boisterous, gregarious and outgoing) while remaining true to the traits that give introverts the upper hand when it comes to success in today's business world.

As technology evolved, a whole new business realm was created. In the '80s and '90s, businesses developed by introverts were becoming mainstream. Men like Bill Gates and Michael Dell are only a few of the introverts that reached phenomenal success during these years. And, the success of introverts was not only limited to the tech boom of the 80's and beyond. The meek were taking the world by storm in a wide variety of industries. With the popularity of the public internet rising in the 1990's, Marc Seriff, Steve Case, and Jim Kimsey hit a big home run with America Online, and by the early 2000s, even more introverts were becoming more and more successful in the tech industry. Mark Zuckerberg began his meteoric rise to wealth with Facebook which opened the door for Noah Glass, Jack Dorsey and others who started Twitter and Kevin Systrom, the founder of Instagram. These people all became phenomenally successful without rising through the ranks of some big company as a successful salesman to one day become the Chief Executive Officer (the success path of the extrovert). They became successful with their intellect. Today, in the late twenty-teens and beyond, there has never been a better time to become a successful introvert. The exponential development of technology will only create more and more opportunities for the quiet and shy to shine.

By now you may be thinking, "Okay, so it's our time. Introvert pride! But how do I crack the code to wealth? How do I capitalize on my introverted tendencies?" Begin by taking an accurate assessment of your strengths. In this book we will discuss a list of common introvert character traits. If they are traits you share, this book will teach you how to make the most of them. If you do not yet possess all the traits in this book, then hopefully the explanation of them may help you unlock them from within.

If you are reading this book, the odds are likely that you believe you are an introvert. In this book, we will discuss some of the common characteristics of introverts and how they can be used to crack the code to wealth. Let's have a look the traits we will be discussing.

Humility: One of the most common misconceptions about humility is that to be humble you have to yourself, or give others undue power over you. The truth is actually quite the opposite. To be humble one must be so sure of one's self that one does not seek out constant praise to feel secure in one's abilities. By the same token, if one is secure enough about the abilities one possesses, and is not so foolish as to believe one can do it all, one learns to take guidance and correction in stride with one's focus purely upon being the best one can be. Introverts' natural tendency to reflect often breeds humility, but if it is a subject with which you struggle this chapter will help you unlock its potential. Humility is strength. In this book, we will show you how to use it to your advantage.

Self-Sufficiency: Another common characteristic of the introvert is the ability to take care of one's self. Because an introvert generally does not like to expose him-or herself to much outside persuasion, the introvert generally develops a strong sense of self-sufficiency. If this is not true of you, the chapter on self-sufficiency will surely inspire you to become more so. If it is one of your strengths already, or once it becomes one of your strengths, this chapter will offer guidance on how to turn self-sufficiency into the ability to gain a position of strength that will allow others to rely on you, in other words, success.

Making the best of solitude: Introverts need to stop often and recharge their batteries. Spending time alone with your own thoughts or allowing your subconscious to process the thousands of bits of information you feed to your brain is an important time for the introvert. (Think of Superman and his fortress of solitude). It may seem like time alone cannot be monetized, as by definition money is a social construct, however, making the best of time spent alone is how an introvert gets ahead. We will discuss in this chapter how to tailor your time alone to become a lone wolf tycoon.

Creativity: Since most introverts spend a lot of time alone, it is important not to waste the time and one common characteristic of the successful introvert is creativity. Whether it be music, painting, writing, gardening, or sculpting most of them find a creative way to spend their time of solitude. If you are introverted, and you dig deep enough, there is likely something within you that ignites passion. Some creative spark dwells within the soul of every introvert and it is all a matter of feeding it fuel to see it take flame. We will discuss ways to apply the lessons learned so far to make sure that your creative endeavors lead to a greater success whether by selling the art you create, playing your music for money or selling the fruits of your garden. If you are not the creative type, this chapter will offer insight into registering the ability to be creative within all of us, and a couple suggestions to help you bring that creativity to the surface. It is important not to waste time even if it is time spent alone.

Being goal oriented: In order to succeed, one must plan to succeed. This is true of everyone. Because introverts spend so much time alone, there is often a lot of contemplation about what he or she wants to do with his or her life. A lot of introverts who are not as creative tend to be more studious and organized, so if your strengths are not in the creative fields, this chapter may feel more your speed. Regardless of where your organizational skills are, steps to outline and pursue your goals will be detailed, and by the end of this chapter, you will have a clear path to success.

Being observant: Because the introvert is, generally speaking, "on the outside looking in" he or she generally gets a better idea of the bigger picture. While the extrovert is busy making themselves the center of attention, the introvert is scanning the room, gauging reactions and making calculations. The applications of this trait reach from being a better team player all the way to knowing exactly which strings to pull to make the puppet dance. The chapter on being observant will help you make the best of your introverted tendency to carefully observe the world around you.

Throughout the chapters, examples will be given of famous

introverts so you know you are in good company. Wisdom from self-proclaimed introverts such as Warren Buffett, Bill Gates, Mark Zuckerburg and J.K. Rowling will be shared to help you set your sights on climbing the heights they have. Inspiration from Albert Einstein and Rosa Parks will show you how even the meek and mild mannered can make impacts on the world that last for generations.

The final chapter of this book will help you maintain success once you have tasted it. It can be overwhelming at times to go from struggling to being successful, and sometimes the path ahead becomes blurry. This chapter's checklist will help you make sure you stay on the path you have set out upon. By the end of this book, you will have all the tools you need to crack the code to wealth and become your very own lone wolf tycoon!

CHAPTER 2

BECOMING BOLDLY HUMBLE

The term "boldly humble" may seem paradoxical, but the truth is that a quiet voice can roar. Humility is often misconstrued as weakness but nothing could be further from the truth. It is a common misconception that to be quiet and still is to be unsure or incapable, but again, this is not always so. Oftentimes one of an introvert's greatest strengths comes from his or her lack of the need to be noticed. Because the introvert gains strength from within, they are less often found tooting the horns of their successes. This is not to say that they do not achieve success, simply that they do so without calling for the spotlight. The introvert is more focused on his or her next success than he or she is on waiting for everyone to acknowledge what he or she has achieved. This is in and of itself an example of how humility can actually speed up the rate of achievements coming to fruition, yet there is more to it than just this.

Being overly confident in one's abilities can lead to disaster.

When one claims greatness to impress a crowd and fails to deliver, how much more negativity ensues for their grandstanding? Working in the shadows to accomplish the thankless may seem less than desirable, but it is in the small, quiet, daily victories that life is lived. The humble man knows that he has worth without having to be told so by others simply because the humble man knows his work is worth doing. To be humble does not mean to not take pride in your work, pride and humility are not mutually exclusive. To be humble is all about recognizing your actual merits, giving yourself credit where credit is due, and not a bit more or less. It is another common misconception about humility that to be humble is to beat yourself down in front of others. Again, nothing could be further from the truth. To be humble is not about downplaying your abilities; it is merely the lack of exaggeration and showboating. You do not have to claim worthlessness - in fact, the act of being successfully humble dispels any doubts as to your worth. To become more and more confident in one's skills and abilities and inherent worth is how one goes from being merely humble to being boldly humble.

An example of bold humility is found in the story of Rosa Parks, a civil rights activist from the mid-1900s. Rosa Parks was not the loudest protester, nor a passionate speech maker, Rosa Parks was in fact widely described as being mild-mannered and meek. While others were fighting for social justice in their own ways, Rosa Parks' security of self set the stage for some of the greatest change to occur in American history. Rosa Parks, a black woman, would not give up the seat she was sitting in to white passengers who had just boarded the bus. She was approached with the ideologies of the time: "you have to move because these white people deserve your seat; they are worth more than you." She politely disagreed, refusing to move, asserting her worth by passively resisting. She did not cause a violent scene when she was taken into custody, it all happened without her making a fuss. Her actions were loud enough, she had no use of loud words. The effects her simple acts have had still echo throughout our society to this day. One woman refusing to sell herself short changed the world.

Rosa Parks was not rich, and she was by no means a tycoon, but she is possibly the best example of how a sure-minded, humble person can make a huge impact on the world. The reality of wealth is that to accrue massive amounts of it, one must change the world. Sometimes, however - as in Rosa Parks' case - that change does not come with monetary wealth attached. It is, nonetheless, notable that the fame of her name has lived for generations, and the worth she created in the minds of some of society's most downtrodden members is not without value. It is, of course, the goal of this book to give you the tools you will need to crack the code to wealth in a financial sense, and to that end, this lesson of humility is still an important one to learn. To be humble, to be securely firm in self-worth without the need to express it constantly, is one of the greatest tools you can take with you into any job. Actions speak louder than words; bragging is a fool's errand. Capability and worth will be determined by your employer, therefore performing your duties diligently and effectively is far more demonstrative of your value to the company than constant self-praise. It is better to be unexpectedly impressive than to fall short of promises made in haste.

Another great example of a humble person with great power and also financial success is Warren Buffet. He is widely considered to be the most successful investor in the world, worth about $66 billion, yet still lives the same humble lifestyle that he did before becoming a billionaire. He has lived in the same house in Omaha NE that he bought in 1958. As an introvert, your inclination will be to stay out of the spotlight. This general sense of humility will keep you from making a fool out of yourself in most situations, but one of the downsides is the fact that it can leave you overlooked. This is where you must learn to be boldly humble. To be boldly humble, you have to build upon the strengths revealed through humility. For example, let's say you have a weekly sales invoice to complete, and because you keep your data organized and are quick at math you consistently turn it in before the end of the day that it is due, never turning it in late. If you procrastinate completing it because you know you can complete it in a short amount of time, your skills are not being showcased. If you were to make sure that the invoice is completed by the night before it is due and then turn it in first thing in the morning, your abilities would begin to shine. After a few weeks of being the first to turn the invoice in, you will begin to stand out among your coworkers. After a few months of consistently turning your work in first, your name will stand out when your employers begin considering who to promote within the company. This example is fairly specific, but the point is universal: act to achieve the best outcomes possible in your line of work and your employers will take note of their own. This is the secret to being boldly humble: you will not have to toot your own horn if others are singing your praises.

CHAPTER 3

SELF-SUFFICIENCY AND BEYOND

Part of being humble, part of being able to be humble, is the ability to take care of one's self. Being self-sufficient, being self-motivated, is another character trait of the introvert that is highly sought after in the professional world. Most bosses do not want to have to micromanage their companies or their employees. They expect that the people they hire to work for them are going to be able to accomplish the tasks they are assigned without having to constantly be checked on. Self-sufficiency in an individual is akin to reliability, and everyone who has people working for them wants to know their team is reliable.

Introverts are known to be mostly self-sufficient. There are rare cases of co-dependent introverts who rely heavily on others for emotional or financial support, but in most cases, the introvert takes care of his or her own needs. The degree to which one is self-sufficient can fluctuate, so one must constantly be reviewing one's needs in order to make sure that they are being met. Realistic self-assessment is key to making sure that one is being efficient in all one does.

Being self-sufficient does not always mean that you have to take care of every aspect of an accomplishment yourself, though. If you go to a restaurant and have a meal cooked for you, but you pay for it with money you have earned, you are still being self-sufficient even though you are not completing every task that needs to be completed. You do not cook the food, you do not wash the dishes, but you get fed because you have earned the money. This network of efficient members—the cook, the dishwashers, the servers—is an example of how when self-sufficient people work together, life goes as planned. This is what employers are looking for: self-sufficiency is akin to reliability, reliability is efficiently effective. Someone who is taking care of their responsibilities will inevitably bring success to their companies.

In truth, self-sufficiency is the first real step one takes to becoming a lone wolf tycoon. Everyone has to start somewhere, and this rung near the bottom is the first one that one must get a grip on to begin one's climb of the corporate ladder. See, if you expect to be able to manage a team, you are going to have to know how to cater to their strengths, weaknesses, and needs. For you to know the strengths and weaknesses of your individual team members, you will have to get to know them, but their needs need not be a puzzle. If you are self-sufficient, you can know what someone needs

TIM L. GARDNER

before they do, because you know what you would need in their situation. For example, let us say you are an oil service technician. You know that to change the oil in a car, you will need certain tools to get the old oil filter off, something to collect the old oil in, a new filter to put back on, and new oil to put into the car. Every car is going to require just a little bit of a tweak of the variables, but the general idea is the same. If you were the self-sufficient kind of person, you would know where each kind of filter is, where the new oil is, and you would make sure to have your tools and collection pan at the ready. A self-sufficient person is an efficient person, you would more than likely have everything you need in an accessible place before you begin your work. This would drastically reduce the time it would take you to complete jobs, meaning you would make your company more money per hour than someone who may never take the time to ensure their space is as streamlined as possible. Remembering to be humble, you would simply be rolling through jobs, continuing to pop up to your bosses with a "Hey, my bay is clear, roll me another one in!" Your bosses would begin to take notice, and you would likely be given instruction in educating your coworkers to be more efficient. You would be tasked with sharing your knowledge of self-sufficiency, and may even be given the responsibility of managing your coworkers to ensure they continue to operate at the standards you hold yourself to. This is, of course, another fairly specific example, but the truth contained is valid: being self-sufficient, paired with being humble, is a fantastic way to ensure that your presence in the workforce is noticed, respected, and eventually strongly desired.

Self-sufficiency does not mean having all the answers either, though. Sometimes it means just being willing to ask the questions. Warren Buffett, the famous philanthropist and financial leader, is an example of a man who recognized his limits, then set out to surpass them. He is a self-professed introvert, yet he is wildly successful in the business realm and became so during a time when business was the extrovert's game. How? Because when he realized he needed to expand his list of abilities, he took it upon himself to register for seminars to learn more about public speaking. He was a man who already had immense talent for sniffing out the best investment opportunities, but he knew that he had areas in which he could improve, so he did just that: improved. His success, fame, and wealth are examples of why you should strive to be as self-sufficient as possible. The term lone wolf tycoon insinuates the ability to take care of yourself, and if ever there was any question as to why, look no further than Warren Buffett's immense success for answers.

CHAPTER 4

SOLITUDE: THE INTROVERT'S BEST FRIEND

If there is one single defining characteristic of the introvert it is that the introvert loves their time alone. While an extrovert gets their energy from being the center of attention, the introvert is no more at home than when he or she is completely alone. Whether it is in your favorite chair with a great new book, or on the couch watching your sixth episode of a new show, or in bed simply browsing social media on your phone or computer, if you are an introvert home truly is where the heart is. It may seem that simply recharging is the best use of your time alone, but if your goal is to become a lone wolf tycoon, cracking the code to wealth will require that you aggressively pursue your empire. This does not mean that you are not to relax and enjoy your time alone, far from it. More often than not, the periods of solitude spent in rest and relaxation are just what you need to get back out there in full force, just remember to never lose focus. We will go over being goal oriented in a future chapter, but in this chapter, we will discuss one of the most beneficial ways to spend your time alone: budgeting. Being humble and self-sufficient are activities that are generally more geared towards your time with others, though they have applications in the solitary times in your life as well. Since we have already discussed these concepts, let's go over how to apply them to your solitude before moving on to discussing how to budget.

There are many ways to define a humble home, ranging from complete deprivation to minimalism, but the most realistic and useful application of being humble at home is to simply live within your means. Can't afford that 60-inch tv? Don't go rent it and pay three times more than it is worth just so you can have it right then and there. Buy yourself something you can afford, and use the lack of everything you cannot afford as the motivation to drive you to get to a financial place where you can afford everything your heart desires. Live as comfortably as possible, and open lines of credit to build your credit, but do not dig yourself holes you cannot get out of just to have the latest gizmos. This is honestly essential if you are going to be a tycoon, lone wolf or not! Money management is pivotal to accruing wealth, so be smart with your money and humble with your home.

On the self-sufficient side of home life, making sure that all your needs are met at home is important to ensure that you will be able to function at your best in society. The introvert recharges his or her batteries at home, so home must be the recharging kind of place. Ensuring that you keep yourself stocked with amenities and plenty of food will ensure that you are able to take care of yourself most properly. A self-sufficient person will make sure all their bills are paid on time and their resources are stocked all times; this will lend the wall which you can press your back to when you need to feel secure. Being self-sufficient will require you to be accurately assessing your situation financially as well, and there is no better place to outline a budget than the comfort of your own home.

Money management is a great way to spend your time alone. Budgeting does not take a long time, but it is something you should be doing frequently throughout the day. When you are alone at home you can do your most hardcore budgeting, but you should be considering it while you are out and about. It is as simple as thinking to yourself "Can I really afford this?" To answer that question most accurately, you will need to develop a budget. Developing a budget is easier than it sounds, and since we have already established its necessity, let's break down exactly how to do it.

To develop a budget, you will need to know how much money you are earning, how much you absolutely have to spend, how much you need to save, and how much that leaves you to play around with. So, plan your month. Let's say you make $2000 a month. Rent is $500; utilities run another $200; food averages $100 a week, so $400 overall; car note and insurance are $320; you put $20 in gas in your car a week, so $80 overall; and your cell phone bill is another $80.

$2000		$500
-		$200
-		$400
-		$320
-		$80
-		$80
$420		

So after all your month's expenses, you have $420 left over to use how you see fit. You should always be putting a little money away for a rainy day, even if it is only $20 a month. If you make $2000 a month and you only save $20 a month, though, you are only saving 1% of your income, which is not a very high amount. At 5%, you are only looking at putting $100 away, and after a year you will have saved $1200 instead of $240. After five years of saving, you could either have $6000 or $1200. Think about it; denying yourself a little extra now could see you giving yourself something major down the line. If you put 10% of your $2000 away a month, after five years you would have $12,000 saved. That's half a year's wages!

After you decide how much you want to save, you can budget the rest of your money by deciding how much you will spend and on what, scheduling movie dates or maybe dinners out, or you can just keep that general number in your mind and be mindful of your spending to ensure you do not over-do it. If you have put away $200 of the $420, you would have $55 dollars a week to spend however you wanted to.

Budgeting is an important part of life, and one best done alone – however, it is not the only way that solitude can be used to get ahead in life. One of the most famous introverts, Albert Einstein, said of solitude: "The monotony and solitude of a quiet life stimulates the creative mind." Einstein has a number of quotes on solitude, and stories of his life never fail to detail the fact that he much enjoyed his solitude. He is even quoted as having said he had a "need for solitude," and it is no wonder why. His ideas, opinions, theories and formulas were groundbreaking, earth-shattering revelations about the world in which we live. His ability to see things in a completely new, yet undeniably true, fashion was a product of the fact that he spent a lot of time by himself deep in thought. His name is synonymous with intellect, so it may seem that his success is unattainable to the average introvert, but the lesson he wanted to share about solitude rings true regardless of how intelligent you may or may not be. His point about the need to be alone is that when you spend time alone you solidify yourself in the knowledge of your own world. This is not to say that you are to live in your own version of reality that is completely detached from the rest of society, it is more to mean that when you spend time thinking for yourself, by yourself, you are able to form your own opinions, ideas and theories about the world around you, maybe even coming up with your own formulas on how to operate within the world. For example, it is well known that social drama spreads quickly by word of mouth. Someone with less information about an event or situation may be inclined to share information as if it were the gospel truth, and that information may sway many minds to form new and more fantastic versions of itself before reaching your ears. If you intake some information that does not seem to register quite right and you sit quietly by yourself thinking about what you already knew and what you have just learned, formulating relativities between what may be and may not be true of both pieces of information, you can eventually form an opinion or theory on the situation that is based more on the truth within your own knowledge and the way you see it in than what has simply been presented to you. Your removal from society's clamoring can allow you the space you need to think, and the ability to form your own opinion or theory on the situation. By then taking your theory back to the population, even if it correlates with another's, you are able to add a personal addition to a public forum that has worth as being of your own creation.

This ability to recalibrate free of the public eye is enjoyed by every introvert. The most successful introverts use the time they spend alone to the fullest of its potential. There are many ways to make sure you are doing so, it will take your own personal reflection on your life to come up with the best way to use your solitude. Cracking the code to wealth is as simple as making the best of absolutely every single moment of your life. Being humble keeps you focused on the reality of what is needed to succeed, which is not constant praise. Self-sufficiency is the mark of a man (or woman) who is taking care of himself (or herself) and will eventually be taking care of others. Time alone can be spent a number of ways, but there are a few things one must do in order to succeed. Budgeting and thinking for yourself are two of the most important aspects of life that you must master if you are to become the most successful lone wolf tycoon. The best time to do either of those things is when you are alone.

CHAPTER 5

MONETIZING CREATIVITY

Most introverts enjoy their time alone because it allows them to express themselves free from the judging eyes of society. Some painters have no problems with letting others watch them work, some even enjoy teaching, but the majority of creative types enjoy exploring their passions in the comfort and solitude of their own homes. Self-expression is a very revealing act, and especially so when one is in the midst of creating a work of art, no matter the medium. It can also be an extremely lucrative experience, as good art fetches high prices. Famous musicians make millions of dollars for performing their music, but even local musicians achieve fame and financial gain by playing their local bars and venues. Master artists fetch millions for their paintings, but even local artists can make a living by painting commissioned pieces if their skills are good enough to be sought after. There are plenty of ways to capitalize on your creativity, let's go over a few.

Because we have expressed the need to be humble quite a bit, and by now you should be getting the point, its application to your creativity will be brief. Do not mistake intent, it is still extremely important to be humble about your work, It is just that by now you should be getting the picture of how important humility is in every aspect of your life. The humble artist's talent is allowed to shine without the taint of his ego. Anyone who is not creative enough to create what may come easily to the artist is naturally going to be a little jealous of their abilities. Left un-fanned, the flames of jealousy soon die down as admiration takes their place. Admiration becomes appreciation, and eventually what they feel for your talents is nothing but positive. If your attitude is pretentious, however, you can almost guarantee that it will have a negative effect on how people receive your artwork. No one likes a braggart, not in an office, not at an art gallery, not at a concert. If you feel like you have a bit of social ineptitude, it is best to just keep quiet and let your art speak for itself. If you play a show but have a tendency to put people off, accept praise with a smile and thanks, and socialize as little as possible. People will appreciate a little mystery a lot more than they would appreciate being talked down to. Again, being humble is all about being appropriate. It is a fine line to walk as an artist; one side craves attention but the other fears rejection. The best bet of making sure your art is the most well received is to let it speak for itself.

Self-sufficiency is an important aspect of introversion that actually has a lot to do with the monetizing of creativity. If you are going to make money off of your artwork, you are generally going to have to be the one putting yourself out there. If you are a musician you may have a bit of help from the rest of the band or a manager, but if you are a visual artist who has piles of paintings stacking up, you will have to take it upon yourself to get your work and your name out there. Luckily, monetizing creativity has never been easier for the introvert. Social media offers many completely free platforms that you can use to showcase your talents. Soundcloud is a free place to upload your music, and Instagram, Facebook, and Tumblr are all free ways to showcase your visual arts. With a little research—something more than familiar to all the self-sufficient—you can find the right way to break into your market.

The most important aspect of being able to capitalize on your creative talents is to never stop creating. J.K. Rowling is an example of how persistently pursuing your talents can lead to unbelievable success. Harry Potter has become one of the most common household names; the world he lives in was entirely fabricated by Rowling. She suffered many failures before penning the books that would skyrocket her to fame and fortune, but she never gave up on her passion. She has often talked about how introverted she is. She tells a story of how she was too shy to ask for a pen when she realized she had forgotten hers while riding a bus. Even though she later became one of England's most famous writers, she started out as a shy mousy bookworm who spent her days daydreaming. The lesson here is that daydreaming is a wonderful pastime when followed with a bit of creative output.

Now, maybe you do not consider yourself the creative type. You may enjoy reading books but could never imagine the possibility of penning the next great novel of our generation. In truth, it is not necessary to set your sights on the top of the mountain if you know you will never reach it. Creativity can be monetized to great success, but it has more value than simply being a way to make money. Creative problem solving is a term used for out of the box thinking in a workplace environment. It is a highly sought after character trait that does not require you to be good with a paint brush, and it is oftentimes found in introverts. The ability to come up with new and inventive ways of solving problems comes from the introvert's natural inclination to consider him- or herself in every situation. An introvert is more likely to consider how he (or she) might solve the problem, and less likely to look for others for guidance. This does not mean the introvert would not take advice, or ask if their solution has been tried before trying it, it just means that they are more likely to consider many options based on how they think they could solve the problem. It requires a knowledge of self to be a creative problem solver because one applies one's experience to a problem. Knowledge of self is very often present in the introvert, therefore they generally make very creative problem solvers.

So you see, creativity comes in many forms. Because of this, there are many ways to apply the concept of creativity in your life. The best way to expand upon your creative abilities is to create. If, again, you do not consider yourself the creative type, do not sell yourself short! Get yourself some puzzles to make in your alone time. While television and books are great ways to present yourself with new situations that you may not have encountered in your life (yet?), allowing you to form complex ideas and opinions based on information you may not have otherwise been exposed to, creative outlets give you time to reflect upon your own life in an engaging and enjoyable way. Puzzles are a great way to create art, as the finished product more often than not is a piece of art. You may not have created the artwork depicted, but spending time putting the puzzle together is a way to exercise those creative problem-solving skills. Finding the right way all the pieces fit is a great brain exercise, and when you have finished your contemplative creation, you can frame your accomplishment and decorate your home with it!

The monetization of creativity is as personal as the experience of being creative. If you are an artist, consider setting yourself up on social media. Research festivals and flea markets you can showcase your work in. Actively pursue the monetization of your talents, no one is going to do it for you! If you are a musician, make demos, visit your local bars and make your face familiar, get yourself on social media as well. The more effort you put into getting yourself out there, the more results you will see! And of course, if you are not the super creative type, explore the concept of creative problem-solving. Doing brain teasing games and challenging yourself with mental exercises like puzzles are great ways to get your creative juices flowing. You may find that the more you consider creative activity the more you find yourself gravitating towards some form of creative outlet. If you get the itch to pick up a guitar, give it a shot! You never know where your fortune may come from, so explore every avenue. Creativity fuels many industries, and the opportunity to break into any of them is only limited by the amount of effort you are willing to put into it. Chase your dreams and you may just catch them!

It should be noted that you should take care not smother your creative flames in the pursuit of living your dreams as a successful artist. Part of being successful at anything comes from the knowledge of when to go full steam ahead, and when to rest and recuperate. Creative endeavors are no different. Do not work yourself into the ground, you will never be successful if you do. Making the best of every moment requires you to accurately assess what needs to be done in each moment. For more on that, let's move on to the chapter on goals and reaching them.

CHAPTER 6

ON GOALS AND REACHING THEM

We have established many character traits that introverts have used to their individual advantages. Humility, self-sufficiency, an affinity for solitude, and creativity are all important pieces of the introvert puzzle. Making sure these pieces fit is achieved by the introvert's natural inclination to being goal oriented. When one knows where one is going, one is far more likely to get there. Success does not happen by accident, and it is generally by careful planning that it is achieved. The general division between the two kinds of people in the world goes "right brain/left brain." Right brain people are said to be more creative, left brain people are more organized and systematic. So, if your strengths are not in the creative fields, take heart; there are still ways to capitalize on your talents!

Setting goals and making schedules are activities that most engage in, but there are those who feel they do not have the time or have no need of looking into the future. A lot of people get wrapped up in the present and life seems to slip by. If you are one of the people who considers schedules out of your grasp (lookin' at you creative types!) never fear! Schedules, like budgets, are easier made than one might expect, and setting goals actually relieves stress.

An important aspect of setting goals that relieve stress is to remain realistic. Humility comes into play when you are making realistic goals that you know you can achieve. Do not set your sights on the moon if you have not built your rocket ship! Setting and achieving realistic goals is of paramount importance when it comes to being the most successful person you can be. Success in every aspect of your life will work towards amassing your wealth; scheduling that success is important to ensuring it occurs!

Being self-sufficient is also important when it comes to maintaining motivation while pursuing your goals. Setting goals for yourself is the first step, attaining those goals will require many steps after it. Keep tabs on yourself to make sure you are accomplishing all that you need to be accomplishing. Nobody else is going to ensure you are working as hard as you can to achieve your goals.

Creativity is applicable to your schedule making in more ways than one. On the one hand, creatively deducing the best course of action could allow for you to come up with avenues of success that others had not considered. On the other, the ability to creatively solve problems as they arise is just as useful! The secret to being successful is not to never fail, it is to persevere through the failures until you reach the finish line. Sometimes this requires a little out of the box thinking, especially when you think you may be completely out of options. If you are the creative type it should come naturally to solve your problems creatively, but even if you are not, an introvert's tendency to spend time alone will oftentimes allot you plenty of time to consider your situation from every angle. The bottom line is this: set goals. From daily goals to three, five, and ten-year plans, setting goals will give you the ability to set your sights on what needs to be done. More likely than not, when you set goals for yourself and begin reaching them, you will find new heights to scale. A perfect example of a successful introvert who continued to achieve his goals, and create new ones, is Bill Gates. Bill Gate's goal was to create both a computer and an operating system that was consumer friendly. These goals were quite lofty during the times that computers filled entire rooms. Bill Gates was known to spend days at a time working on his computers with his team, forever coming up with new and improved ways of transmitting data. His legacy today is a testament to the heights to which anyone, introverted or extroverted, can climb with enough determination to achieve their goals. To this day, Bill Gates is investing in companies he sees worth in, giving to charities he believes in, and his company continues to produce software that allows billions of people to use their computers to their fullest potential. His impact on the world is substantial, and it all came from him having goals and sticking to them.

Make a five-year plan for yourself. You do not have to write it down, but keep it in mind. Think into your future; where do you want to be in five years? What sort of job would you like to have? How much money would you like to be making? How are you going to achieve these goals? When you start working backward from the future, you can turn your long term abstract goals into the daily schedule which you will need to follow to achieve those goals. That part you may want to write down.

Get yourself a planner and keep up with it. If your phone has a planner function, take advantage of it! Set alarms for yourself to remind yourself to exercise when you should be exercising every day. Make sure to put all your appointments into your phone or your planner so that you do not double book yourself or show up late. Keeping track of your life with diligence is the only way to ensure your success, so keep a schedule! After a certain time of planning your life, your physical reminders will fade from necessity as the habits will become parts of your daily life, but you still need to make sure that you are keeping some sort of calendar of your appointments. And make sure to schedule yourself down time! One of the worst parts of spending time doing "nothing" is the feeling that there is "something" that you should be doing. If you keep a schedule, one of the unsung joys is the ability to check off all the things you need to do, leaving you with nothing to do eventually. When you have done all you need for the day you get to enjoy the rewards of your hard work, namely the ability to relax and be comfortable in the home you work to maintain. By keeping your schedule, you end your days feeling accomplished instead of worried. You can also pencil in downtime throughout the day if you know you will be working long hours. When you have projects to get done, scheduling them in sections can help to keep from becoming overwhelmed. The benefits of scheduling are far reaching, so grab yourself some form of planner and get to it! As for your long-term goals, remember to keep them achievable. The trick to achieving long-term goals is to set yourself plenty of short term goals. When you continuously complete your short-term goals, you not only make sure that you stay on the right path, but you give yourself little victories to celebrate. When you do accomplish goals, it is important to take the time to celebrate your successes. It may seem inconsequential to celebrate simple accomplishments, or maybe even a little pretentious, but the truth of the matter is that celebrating your short-term accomplishment lends credibility to the value of your long-term goals. If you gain real joy from completing your short-term goals, the long-term goal you have planned for yourself will be even more exciting, and the time you spend grinding towards it will be all the more worth it. If you find that you are not enjoying your accomplishments as much as you had expected to, it can give you an idea as to what you can expect once you reach the finish line. If you have to make a career change, better to do so as soon as you realize that the field you have chosen is not the right fit for you. Celebrating your little victories need not be anything grand, but the joy you feel should be allowed to flow. Indulging yourself in it will lend you strength on the dark days, so do not be afraid to get excited with yourself!

Another secret to amassing wealth is to genuinely enjoy what you do. The joy you feel when you are doing something you genuinely enjoy is a reward in and of itself, but when you do what you love for a living, there is a better chance you will pour your whole heart into it, and that shines through. Whether it is a creative endeavor or a sales invoice, someone who is enjoying doing what they are doing will be noticed. If you have to do things you don't enjoy, as is often the case, just make sure that you are set upon a path to eventual joy. Planning your goals and scheduling your life is how you make sure that you end up where you want to be, and everyone agrees that regardless of where they eventually end up, they want to be happy.

CHAPTER 7

FROM OBSERVATION TO IMPLEMENTATION

One of the most commonly described traits of an introvert comes from their interactions in social environments. It is often said of introverts that they seem to be scanning the room, taking it all in, watching and analyzing everyone. This is generally true of most introverts in social situations, as they are unlikely to be engaged in boisterous laughing or light-hearted conversation. The introvert's natural inclination is to stay in the background, observing everything around them and making calculations as to how best to proceed. This trait has led to many a great invention by introverts, most namely Facebook.

That's right, Mark Zuckerberg, CEO of Facebook is quite possibly the most famous introvert of this generation. Warren Buffett, Bill Gates, Mark Zuckerberg: the titans of their time. How did Mark Zuckerberg come up with his genius social media site? By observing a need and an opportunity, and taking it upon himself to seize the opportunity to fill that need. His social media site was developed with a tiny group of programmers to connect college students at the college he attended. His ingenuity in bringing the old campus tradition of a "face book" to the new computer age was soon adopted by colleges all across the country. Eventually, the invitation-only platform began allowing the invitation of college preparatory high schools, and soon after the whole world was connecting with Facebook, and Zuckerberg became a billionaire.

He saw a need, he filled the need. He saw the opportunity, he seized the opportunity. The ability to do this came from his introverted tendency to observe the world around him. In a world that seemingly has a new major app coming out every day, it may seem like every need is being filled, that every opportunity has been seized. Facebook seems like it came out of nowhere and conquered the social media realm, but in fact, it was once a competitor itself. Myspace and Xanga were very popular social media sites, with more customization features and less exclusivity than Facebook, yet Facebook managed to surpass them all in popularity over time. So if you have observed a way that you can fill a need, do not be discouraged by the fact that others are trying to do so as well. The market is unpredictable; if you pour yourself into your work you have just as much a shot as anyone else trying to make it.

As an introvert, you may notice that your natural tendency is to observe the world around you. The world around you is filled with opportunities yet to be discovered or things that can be done in a different way. When you observe these things, look at them as opportunities and consider how you can take advantage of them. It is okay to start small. Every opportunity is not a billion dollar idea. Is there a store in your neighborhood that doesn't carry a product that you would like to buy? Is it something that you can provide?

Rick Malley is not a famous man, but he is an introvert who used his powers of observation to start a successful small business. He was a bellhop at a local hotel on the Mississippi gulf coast who enjoyed to garden as a hobby. He was planting his spring garden and wanted to buy a specific type of pepper so he went to the local garden center and tried to purchase the plant only to learn that they did not carry that particular type of pepper plant. He tried several other local stores only to find that no one in the region carried the plant. After some research to make sure the plant would, in fact, grow in the climate where he lived he went to the local grocery store and purchased a few of his favorite peppers and after using them for cooking, he saved the seeds. There were several hundred seeds and after some research, he planted the seeds and the next thing he knew, he had several hundred small pepper plants. He took the plants to the local garden center and they bought them all. The idea worked and now he grows plants from seeds and sells them to local garden centers and other stores in his region.

This is just one example of something small that turned into a thriving business because of one person's ability to observe and implement. Following through is the key. If Rick had simply accepted the fact that his favorite pepper plant was not available in his area and bought something else instead, he would have never started a small business. Instead, he did something about it. He observed and implemented. As an introvert, your natural tendency to quietly observe is a blessing. Observation without implementation will get a person nowhere, but making an observation and taking action can lead a person anywhere.

As an introvert, your observation skills can be the perfect second set of eyes. Where most people can look at a situation or a set of problems over and over again without seeing a solution, the introvert's observation skills set them apart. Even the most observant, when faced with the same problem they have been considering for a while, begins to lose the ability to see new ways to solve their problems. Sometimes, consultants are hired to come in to fix problems because they are a new set of eyes on an old problem. Are you an ideal consultant? If you have an area of expertise, consulting may be the perfect career path for you as an introvert! A consultant does not have to spend a lot of time around large groups of people; they come in when they are needed, and they get out when they are done. A consultant's expertise is oftentimes unquestioned; if you are a good consultant your ideas will be appreciated enough by your clients to stand on their own merit, word will be passed throughout the industry by people who are impressed with what you do, and you will be able to be humble in your line of work and still be recognized. Being a consultant is one of the most self-sufficient career path choices one can make; their lifestyle is literally the monetization of their ability to fix problems. As was already mentioned, the come and go lifestyle of a consultant perfectly fits the introvert's desire to spend a considerable amount of their time in solitude. Also, if creative problem solving is your specialty, then being a consultant is again the perfect job for you! Being goal oriented and being able to schedule well is another talent that lends itself to a successful consulting business. A lot of times consultants will be hired because companies have fallen behind in their schedules and they need someone with powerful observational skills to help them realistically adjust their expectations.

Take a look at the world around you. What do you notice? Have you ever thought or told a friend that "they should" or "there should be" because you have observed a need? If you have, then you have observed without implementing. Put those observation skills to work for your success and you are on the way to cracking the code to success.

CHAPTER 8

MANAGING YOUR SUCCESS

Once you crack the code to wealth, you are going to want to keep it. As you find yourself rising to higher levels of success financially and in other aspects of your life, it is important to understand how to stay there and continue to grow both financially and emotionally. Here are some important steps to ensure your success has a long shelf life:

Do not isolate yourself. You may only have a few relationships, but they will be deep and meaningful. Work on building deep relationships with your family and friends and from time to time, add new relationships to your life. Personal relationships are as important as business relationships in maintaining a healthy life. By developing relationships in your business world, you may find that you are finding it easier to build relationships in your personal life. Of course, as an introvert, you are going to like your time alone, but make sure you spend good times with other people from time to time. Humans are social creatures by nature, and to have the healthiest life, one must not isolate one's self completely.

Take care of your health. This is true of everyone but can be especially tricky to the introvert. Because the introvert does not like to spend too much time in public settings, especially around high energy people, a gym might be the last place you find an introvert. If you find that gyms are too intimidating for you, you will need to find other ways to keep your health up. Meditation and yoga can help you to stay mentally focused and healthy. Jogging is another way to stay fit. If you want to try to make it to the gym, try putting on headphones and see if that helps isolate you enough to make it through a workout routine. Dieting is another important factor to consider. Even if you do not want to get too into dieting, you need to watch what you eat. A balanced diet is better than nothing, even if you are not counting calories.

Always seek to improve yourself. Take time for education and honing your craft. Warren Buffett's example of taking courses to further his education in areas that he was less skilled in is one you should take to heart. If you feel you have mastered one area of your craft, focus your attention on a new one. There is never a shortage of information these days, so never stop learning! Do not limit yourself to only learning about things you feel are related to your work either. If you get a wild idea to learn a completely new hobby, explore the thought! If you wake up one morning with a strong desire to paint, but no idea how to begin, research it! You may be as skilled as you need to be at work, but you can never know too many ways to have fun!

Be kind to yourself. You are probably your worst critic. If you are an artist or musician, especially so. If you find yourself encountering failure on your road to success, try not think too long about them, only long enough to learn the lesson and move on. You are doing the best you can, and that is all anyone can ask. Nobody ever got anywhere because they beat themselves up enough. Learning from your mistakes is important, but beating yourself up is not the way to do so.

Give yourself credit for your successes. As an introvert, others may overlook your because you are not seeking the spotlight, and extroverts may intentionally step in front of you into the light, but always give yourself credit and your work will speak for itself. This is how you manage to become boldly humble. By quietly congratulating yourself on your successes, your own appreciation of yourself makes you work harder, which in turn creates more and more successes. Even if it does not happen right away, you will eventually be given the credit you deserve by others if you continue to give it to yourself.

Build a team. Unlike extroverts who need all the credit, introverts understand the value of a team. Build a strong team and keep them happy. Working together may not be your natural inclination, but it may be in the best interest to your success. Bill Gates does not run Microsoft alone. Find a good team to work with to accomplish your goals, and you will climb the ladder of success much faster.

Communicate. More often than not, introverts are constantly talking to themselves. This inner dialogue is a part of why introverts feel so much more comfortable alone, their minds are always going. The downside to this inner dialogue is that sometimes it does not make its way out. Learn to communicate the important parts of your inner dialogue with your team, and your customers or clients. It is important they are kept up with what you have going on in your head, and since they cannot be in there with you, you have to talk it out with them.

Be accessible. Set aside time to be accessible to your team and to your customers. Remember your planner? If you are to be successful in life, you have to make sure that what you are doing is having its desired effect. The only way you will know it is doing so is if you make the time to hear back from the people involved in it. If your team has problems, or successes, to report, they need to be able to reach you at any time. If your customers have complaints or compliments, they also need to be able to be responded to in a timely manner. Having a business email is a good way to ensure that you are able to respond to everyone who needs your attention, so consider getting one.

Carve out time for solitude. As you become more and more successful, solitude will become harder to find. The constant demands of a successful business will also create a greater demand for your time. Be careful not to sacrifice solitude. At the same time that accessibility is important, your battery recharging solitude is also very important. Do not sacrifice all of your alone time, as an introvert it will lead to you being less capable in the times you are in public, and that will not make anything better for anyone.

Identify and stay connected with your support network. As an introvert, you are going to be generally more inclined to have a small network of people who you consider close. These people are going to mean a lot to you, though, and making sure that you are connected to them will become more and more important the more successful you become. It will also become more difficult as your time is needed for more and more business related matters. Just remember to stay connected to the people who were there for you when you were down, and the people who continue to be there for you when life gets rough. These people will also be the ones who celebrate your successes with you the most genuinely, so stay connected with them. It may seem mildly against your introverted tendency to be self-sufficient, but having a support group is important. Being self-sufficient means taking care of your own needs, but that is not always possible. You would not be able to perform your own open heart surgery, sometimes you are not able to solve every one of your problems.

Learn to deal well with any setbacks that may occur. If things are not working out as planned, make sure you are not beating yourself up, but also make sure you are learning the best way to move forward. Learning to deal with setbacks is more than just emotional damage control. You need to be solving problems creatively if you are going to be successful. Sometimes taking a step back from it all may be necessary, sometimes a problem will require you to take a harder look at what you are doing. Being adaptable to your situations will be the best way to make sure you come up with the best solutions.

Review your goals, set new ones if necessary. The process of setting goals for yourself should be a constant thing in your life. You do not make one grocery list in your life, you should not make only one list of goals. As you continue to grow, as time passes and you reach your goals, you should be always setting your sights on new horizons. Every hill you climb should give you a new mountain to consider. If you are to become a lone wolf tycoon, you can never be satisfied with where you are. This does not mean you cannot appreciate your hard work, it just means that you must stay hungry for success no matter how much of it you may have your fill of.

Share your goals and the progress you have made in reaching them. There is a better chance that you will reach your goals if you have shared them with your support network. The idea is not to brag constantly about what you plan and what you do, the idea is simply to let those in your support group know about what you have going on in your life. Sharing your goals with others gives you not only motivation to stay focused, but it allows others the opportunity to give you valuable input in ways they see that you could improve. As we discussed in the chapter about being observant, an outside pair of eyes can often times see solutions that a pair who is super focused cannot. The same is true of your goals, someone close to you may have valuable insight to share on them, so keep them informed!

Print out your goals. Printing your goals out, or writing them down, is a great way to turn these intangible ideas of the future into real world existences you can see and touch. Even though they are just words on paper, they are far more emphasized when they are physically in front of you. Make a few copies of your list of goals and hang them in places around your house that you will easily see and they will be quick reminders to keep you motivated in moving forward. Hanging them on the bathroom mirror is a great place, or on the fridge, or on your bedroom door. It may sound silly, but constantly reading your goals really can help to keep you focused.

Cracking the code to wealth will not happen overnight. It will take time, perseverance, and dedication. Make sure you are keeping yourself motivated. If you find it hard to keep yourself motivated, establish a support group to help keep your motivated. There will be times where you feel like giving up on your goals, this is another time the support group will come into play. Cracking the code to wealth is not easy, or everyone would do it. It will beat you down, you have to keep getting back up. Eventually, with enough hard work and determination, and a little good luck, you will find yourself becoming the lone wolf tycoon.

CONCLUSION

Thank for making it through to the end of The Introvert Love & Wealth Bundle. Let's hope it was informative and able to provide value to you with all of the tools you need to achieve your goals in love, and cracking the code to wealth. If you had any doubts about the ability of the introvert to become wildly successful, then hopefully this book has dispelled them. An introvert is only limited by his or her willingness to succeed. As you have learned throughout this book, an introvert is just as set up to succeed, if not more so, than any extrovert.

The next step is to begin setting your goals, making your budgets, and working towards becoming a quiet cupid and lone wolf tycoon!

There's that old cliché: "Rome was not built in a day". The same is as true for your lone wolf business empire as it was for the Roman Empire so long ago. Inevitably, your empire will take time and dedication for you to see it to fruition. It will take patience, talent, and – admittedly – a fair amount of luck. However, if you make sure to make the best of your introvert character traits, you will have a firm foundation to build upon. There's no telling how prosperous and fortunate you could be with a simple combination of a strong foundation, some essential skills, a keen eye for niche opportunities, and a lot of patience, but all signs point to "very". I wish you luck on your journey to become the best lover and businessperson you can be – not in spite of your introversion, but rather by taking full advantage of it.

If you like to hear about my future projects, please visit the address below.

http://clika.pe/l/13430/56723/

Finally, if you found this book useful in any way, a review on Amazon is always appreciated!

Following is an excerpt from my first book The Disciplined, Resilient Child. Try this sample, and if you like it, feel free to grab it on kindle, paperback, or audiobook.

The Disciplined Resilient Child

21 Tips To Get Your Child To Be Respectful, Responsible, And Resilient For a Successful Future

CHAPTER 1

INTRODUCTION - BUILDING STRONGER, RESPECTFUL AND RESPONSIBLE KIDS

Someone wise once said, "It takes an entire village to raise a kid." That wasn't too way off considering how much effort goes into bringing up kids, teaching them sound values, and molding their personality. We all want that happy, compassionate, well-adjusted and talented kid, who will turn out to be a wonderful adult.

Human personality evolves each day. Just look at your social media feed if nothing else for evidence. It is filled with cutesy babies and toddlers hitting significant milestones and doing adorable things. Personalities are formed as toddlers interact with other toddlers on the playground or mingle with adults or when they win a game or even when they learn to play a musical instrument.

Scary as it sounds, your child's personality is being molded every waking minute, whether you like it or not whether you intend it or not. They are watching, observing, assimilating and learning.

A child can assume fairly well developed traits or some personality at 7 years of age. In some cases, it could also be as early as 4-5 years of age. However, the very nature of personality is dynamic. It is not a static quotient, and as such, there is a typical and unique trait framework in each of us, our personalities keep evolving. As an individual matures, there are constant changes in their personality due to training, peer groups, experiences, and other crucial factors.

However, personality is more dynamic, their core values remain more or less the same. What we learn during our most formative years is what stays with almost forever as a template on which traits are built and brought down.

From 3 to 5 years, kids get comfortable with the idea of expressing themselves verbally, according to the author and psychology expert of Parenting Stress, Kirby Deater-Deckard. They learn to slow down a bit when they get hyper enthusiastic, scared or sad. Children at this age boast of greater attention and lesser emotional reaction. This is the age where kids are slowly building their confidence, while developing skills on how to treat others.

Gradually, they start learning how to show concern for their loved ones, while also slowly coming into their own, unique personality. They start understanding concepts of sensitivity and respect, along with the fact others have feelings and requirements too (mom needs to sleep too). Kids typically start displaying more affection, and create a fantasy life at 5-6 years of age. This is where they yo-yo between being highly demanding and affectionately cooperative.

Each child differs from another in wonderful ways. Budding personalities, discipline enforced at home/school, experiences, peer groups, and more contributes towards building a healthy and well-adjusted personality. By being sensitive, conscious and responsive to their unique strengths and weakness, we foster healthier personalities.

Other than vital social skills such as conflict resolution, imagination development, team work, decision making, standing up for their rights, creating, leading, exploring and more, we also need them to have their core traits such as respect, responsibility and resilience sorted. These will be the key traits that will build their interpersonal relationships, their attitude towards life's challenges and their work.

So how exactly does one build a respect, resilience and responsibility in 2-12 year olds? How can adults contribute towards disciplining their children for a successful and happy future? Well, it does begin early. Here are 21 proven tips for getting your precious little one to be a shining example of respect, responsibility and resilience.

CHAPTER 2

7 EXPERT TIPS FOR TEACHING YOUR CHILD RESPECT

E mpowering your child by teaching them the value of respect is probably the best gift you can give them. The stark reality is that it isn't an all bed of roses process, since children do not come with a pre-installed respect mode (much like every other thing they learn). It isn't something that's going to happen naturally or organically. It has to be taught to them through words, examples and behavior.

Respect is the natural basis for compassion, selflessness, considerateness and empathy. Therefore, teaching your child respect lays the foundation several other social traits that lead to them growing up into socially adjusted, happy and helpful folks. Here are some brilliant ways to instill respect in your child.

1. Don't Nose Dive to Their Level

In a bid to give them a taste of their own medicine, a lot of parents make the mistake of talking down to their child or treating them in a disrespectful manner. This is parenting blasphemy. There is no need to go to their level when they pout or throw annoying temper tantrums. When you mirror their behavior, they aren't likely to show you much respect, which only ends up worsening an already trying situation.

Think carefully before you speak. Is this going to get your child to be more respectful? Does this indicate your respect for other people? If the ideas don't sound good enough to get your kid to respect people, drop it. There isn't a 'let's even out the scores' match going on here. You are the parent, which means you set the benchmark for them, not allow them to set a benchmark for your behavior (makes sense?).

When your little one is being disrespectful, stay away from the temptation of using the same words, gestures and behavior patterns. Be firm by all means that this isn't acceptable behavior, however don't imitate it. This only reinforces the disrespectful behavior in child's eye. Remember, everything you do (the good and bad) is a validation for the child. Your bad behavior will only serve to encourage them for following suit.

Instead of getting all worked up, try and move away from the area to spend some time getting over what the child said, and plan your next move. Be assertive, yet loving and respectful to teach your child the art of treating others with respect. This way they are likelier to realize their folly, own up and start mending their ways. The more you push them, the more they'll bounce. So stop treating them the way they treat you, if it's wrong because two wrongs are never going to make a right.

2. Respect Your Partner

How to talk to and treat your partner sets the basis for your child's future relationship dynamics. Parents often make the grand fallacy of trying to teach their kids respect while subtlety encouraging/validating disrespectful behavior by talking down to their partner. If you want to set the tone for respect within your children, let them see their parents treat each in a respectful manner. Being respectful towards your partner doesn't mean you do not have any differences. You can have differences, but set standards for disagreeing so your child knows it is alright to differ but disrespect is not acceptable.

Keep your fights clean. Avoid indulging in name calling, personal attacks or raking up past scores just to get even with your partner. Be conscious about how you conduct your disagreements, especially when the child is around. Keep it healthy, logical and balanced. Try to divert the disagreement/argument towards a solution.

3. Establish Rules

Set boundaries to make children realize that the world doesn't function according to their fancy, and that they have to display consideration for others. Also, if they find it tough to follow rules at home, there's little hope of them being able to respect authority in school. Allowing them to behave as if the entire planet revolves around them, without holding them accountable for their actions is a sure-shot stage for future failure.

Don't just set rules and expect them to toe the line. Talk to them about why exactly these rules are in place, and their importance. Stick these rules prominently, where the children can spot it. You can also draw them together to make it more fun and interesting for the child.

Don't expect them to have an immediate connection with the rules or understand the value of respect. Break it into bits and pieces, and allow them to chew just enough for them to swallow and not choke themselves.

Teach them the value for showing consideration for others in little things. For instance, leaving their toys around make seem totally harmless to them but it creates a messy environment for others. Talk to them about the consequences of breaking rules. Keep repeating and reinforcing these rules periodically, and be prepared to make them face the consequences whenever necessary.

Establish clear limits to make it easy for children to understand exactly what is expected for them. If you want the child to follow a particular behavior pattern (saying please, thank you etc.), ensure you are consistent with your reminders and rewards/reprimands.

4. Teach Them to Listen to Others

Your child comes excitedly from school to tell you about how little Tommy fought with another boy or the lovely paper bird they made in craft class today. You are busy on your phone, typing furiously while the little one is talking. Guess, what message you are unknowingly sending them? They don't deserve your time or attention. You don't value them enough to listen to them.

Lack of interest or response when someone is talking can be one of the most subtle yet worst forms of disrespect. Appearing distracted, not making eye contact, fiddling with your phone, lack of response are no eye contact are signs of not respecting the speaker enough to acknowledge what they are saying. Your kid is picking up all the clues. This is exactly how they are going to treat others who talk to them.

Train your child to be a courteous and well-mannered conversationalist. Ask them not to interrupt until someone has finished speaking. Educate them about the importance of waiting for their turn to speak rather than hijacking every conversation. This instills a strong sense of consideration and respect for others.

You can practice this with your child, while having meaningful conversations. Do a role-paly. Play the habitual interrupter or disinterested listener, and allow your child to experience how it feels when no one listens to them. Practice keen listening skills such as acknowledging the other person's words or following up with a question or keeping your body language attentive. Your children will invariably get into the habit of listening to people. Isn't it amazing how all parents want to teach their children to talk, and no one wants to teach them to listen?

Children are easily distracted these days, what with all the smart phones and shiny gadgets. As parents ensure that you lead by example, teach your child the value of stopping whatever they are doing to look at the person speaking to them in the eye. We inculcate this habit by stopping and putting down our phones when our children speak to us. Parents convey more through their actions than mere words. Teach young ones to acknowledge people when they visit you. They should raise and greet people who come home. Children can also be taught to initiate conversation by saying something polite like, "Hi! How has your day been?"

You can also teach your child not to interrupt a conversation you are having with someone else. Teach them some clever strategies when they are bubbling with excitement and want to talk to you immediately. They can put their hand on your shoulder and wait for a conversation pause before saying, "excuse me" and entering the conversation politely.

5. Encourage a Spirit of Open-Mindedness

Being respectful towards others involves a fair share of getting to know them well and understand where they are actually coming from. You may obviously not get along with everyone you meet but it is important to make it clear to our children that though they are not under any obligation to like everyone, and that not everyone will be like how they are, they have to treat people with respect. It is alright to not take to everyone instantly, but they shouldn't be allowed to treat people badly just for being different.

Educate your child to be open-minded at the onset. This trait will serve them wonderfully well in life. Teach them to be respectful towards other cultures, traditions, and interests. Let them try multiple activities, mingle with different sets of children and try fresh activities periodically. Allow them to forge new connections.

Kids display a quick judgmental tendency. They instantly decide they are incompatible with someone after talking for some time. However, as a parent, you can gently point it out to them that though someone is different from them or doesn't share their interest, the person deserves their kindness. Teach them the golden value of agreeing to disagree (so vital in the social media age).

Instill in them the idea that their way of doing things isn't the only right way. So, if John doesn't like ketchup on everything and you love it, John isn't weird or any lesser than you. He's just different, and both the ways are great. It is alright to love and hate ketchup. You're teaching your child to respect different ways of doing things even when these don't necessarily match their way. These are the kind of children who grow up to be awesome problem solvers and peacemakers in later years, and we know the world needs more than a few of these, don't we?

Kids are pros at spotting differences in others who aren't like them, and will often mention it too. When someone looks, dresses and behaves differently from them, they notice it instantly. These moments can often be embarrassing for you as a parent. To avoid it, start early when it comes to educating your child about diversity, and how to embrace differences gracefully.

One of the biggest mistakes parents make it silencing or dismissing their child when they say something that doesn't reflect sensitivity for people who are different from them. Instead of shushing the child, address the issue right away with confidence and assertiveness. Don't be all embarrassed and tongue-tied. If your child has said something impolite about others, apologize to them right in front of him/her and go on to educate them about the diversity.

Teach them that not everyone is the same, and that's not a

negative thing. Use the curiosity triggered opportunity to educate your child about celebrating differences. One of the best ways to achieve this is exposing them to multiple cultures and traditions. Exposure to a broad variety of backgrounds makes them more receptive to people who are different from them.

One of the best strategies to achieve this is to allow the child to take pride in their cultural roots, yet celebrate other cultures too. Help your little one trace his family origins. Let him/her derive a powerful sense of pride about his/her ancestral roots. How about organizing a multi-cultural party, where every child can wear their ethnic costume or bring along a family specialty food. Invite friends over for such unique birthday and cultural celebrations to help them appreciate each other's unique way of life.

A fun way to do this by ensuring they watch shows and read books that feature characters from different backgrounds. You can also encourage real interpersonal interactions with people from different backgrounds. Help them experience various cuisines or participate in a cultural event (belonging to a different ethnicity) in your neighborhood.

There are so many fun ways through which you can introduce your child to newer cultures and experiences with the intention of making them more appreciative and respectful towards people who are different from them.

An expert tip to get your child to respect difference is to help them look beyond the differences to what they also share in common with others, and how at a larger level everyone is the same.

For example, tell them how the girl wearing the headscarf is just as much a skating buff as them or how someone with a different accent is as much as ice-cream lover as them. This makes them view everyone with a sense of universality and uniformity, and instantly overlook the differences to feel a sense of oneness with other children. They learn to establish connections with people who are different, and this paves the way for greater respect.

Also, teach them to respect authority and disagree respectfully if they have to. Let them know that while it is alright to disagree with a teacher politely, it isn't alright to embarrass those in authority publically. They can always wait until after class to discuss the issue with their teacher.

Teach children to treat others the way they expect to be treated by other people. This encompasses many situations, however as a golden rule it teaches them that everyone is important and deserves to be treated with respect, compassion and dignity.

Children automatically become more excited and receptive towards different experiences, which in turn introduce them to a world brimming with exciting new possibilities. That is a wonderful payoff, isn't it?

6. Small Acts of Respect Add Up

Teach your child to be respectful and considerate of other's things by inculcating habits such as always seeking permission before using something that doesn't belong to them. Even if it is something that belongs to you or the child's sibling, teach them to ask before using it. If there's a designated dinner table seat for each member, encourage the child to seek permission before sitting on someone else's seat. Similarly, they should be trained to proactively demonstrate small gestures of respect and considerateness. For instance, if you are surfing a site on the computer and the child is sitting on the chair, they should immediately offer the chair to you or bring another chair for you to sit. These seemingly tiny acts go a long way in teaching them to think and care for others, and not just themselves.

When your child fills their cup with water, teach them to ask others if they'd like to have water too. This will invariably turn them into an adult who respectfully ask others what they'd like to have when they go pick up a take-away as grown-ups. Children can be taught to grow up with more sensitive, considerate and reverent traits.

Teach them to be perceptive and responsive to other people's needs. Small gestures such as holding doors for people, letting them walk before you, and treating everyone well at home, school and public places can go a long way in building their character for future.

Sometimes we tend to let kids go scot free with teasing and being insensitive towards one another, especially among siblings. Teach them the value of respecting their buddies and siblings just like adults do. Tell them firmly that when someone says no, it means no, and when someone says stop, they have to respect the person's wishes and stop right away. While this may seem pedestrian, children should always learn to say, "Yes Ma'am" or "Thank you Sir" along with "please", "excuse me" and "sorry." They shouldn't be going around with a feeling of entitlement. Their words and body language should always convey politeness, manners and gratitude.

7. Avoid Overreactions

If you overreact and give your child's act of disrespect more attention than it deserves, you are indirectly encouraging them to behave badly to grab your attention. The temptation to raise your voice and express your displeasure can be hard to resist, however this does little to teach your child respect. This may even validate the idea that it alright to scream when you're angry or upset.

When you find your child acting in a disrespectful manner, take him aside and state quietly but assertively that ordering people around is not how it works here. Teach him to ask respectfully when he wants something. You are setting a calm, firm and respectful example for your child to emulate. At the same time, you aren't embarrassing the child or overacting.

If your child acts disrespectfully in public or has been particularly disrespectful off late, don't throw a full blown tantrum in public or they'll follow suit. Instead, wait to discuss the situation later. Ask your little one what's going on or why he/she felt so upset?

They could be acting particularly frustrated due to a reason, and discussing it may help you make it easier for the child rather than simply reprimanding him/her. Inquire with your child to understand if there's something you are missing. You may be failing to read between the lines, and this could be causing even more frustration/conflict within the child's mind.

Check if they need more time with you or if they want to talk to you about something. Help them negotiate their fears, insecurities and frustrations. This can make them calmer, more balanced and less snappy/disrespectful all the time. Sometimes, all you need is a bit of understanding and cupcakes (okay, I just made that up).